POND PUDD
AND SUSSEX SMOKIES
SUSSEX'S FOOD AND DRINK

KEVIN NEWMAN

AMBERLEY

For Laura and Carol with love – two Sussex women whose culinary efforts have made me the (slightly chubby) man I am today.

The Downs are Sheep, the Weald is corn, you be glad you are Sussex born!
Rudyard Kipling, 'The Run of the Downs'

Apples be ripe
Nuts be brown
Petticoats up
Trousers down.
(An 'old Sussex folk song' according to Spike Milligan in *Adolf Hitler: My Part In His Downfall*)

First published 2021

Amberley Publishing
The Hill, Stroud
Gloucestershire, GL5 4EP

www.amberley-books.com

Copyright © Kevin Newman, 2021

The right of Kevin Newman to be identified as the Author of this work has been asserted in accordance with the Copyrights, Designs and Patents Act 1988.

Bottom left cover image courtesy of Ewan Munro under ShareAlike 2.0 Generic.

ISBN 978 1 4456 9706 2 (print)
ISBN 978 1 4456 9707 9 (ebook)

British Library Cataloguing in Publication Data.
A catalogue record for this book is available from the British Library.

Typesetting by SJmagic DESIGN SERVICES, India.
Printed in Great Britain.

Contents

A grand display of Sussex food in the past. (Courtesy of Royal
Pavilion and Museums, Brighton and Hove – RPAM BAH)

Introduction

As a county whose wealth, health and happiness were originally largely dependent on fishing and farming until its establishment as a tourist destination, it is no surprise that Sussex's food and drink have played – and still play – an important role. Still today a predominantly rural county, Sussex is still a vital part of the UK's agricultural sector, with fishing boats bringing their catches back to our harbours and up onto the beaches of Hastings, Worthing and others. In recent years, Sussex has been part of the micro- and craft-brewery boom and its south-facing fields are dotted with successful and critically acclaimed vineyards – something never expected a generation ago. It is therefore now even seen as the home (or at least the epicentre) of British wine production, and our cheese (such as Brighton Blue) has won awards at the World Cheese Awards. Producing

Fishing still taking place on the beaches of Hastings today.

This 1760s picture of Brighton before most major development shows the town's reliance on fishing and farming from its pre-resort days. (Courtesy of RPAM BAH)

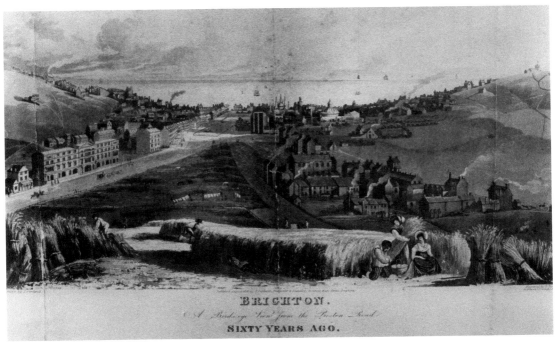

Early view of Brighton with haymaking in foreground. (Courtesy of RPAM BAH)

Upperton Vineyard, West Sussex.

good, locally sourced food is the key to a great Sussex pub and restaurant today, but we can still be found participating in centuries-old traditions with links to food and drink. One example is Lewes Bonfire Night, where the most famous Protestant martyr out of all the seventeen it commemorates, Derek Carver, was burned on the orders of Mary I – in a beer barrel to mock his 'lowly' profession. Wine has been made in Sussex since the Romans, and with the Harvey's brewery in Lewes we have one of the country's oldest (and more importantly, still independent and family-run) breweries.

I am delighted to write a book on Sussex's imbibing and nibbling past, partly as food and drink (whether producing, eating and drinking or celebrating it) runs through the county's DNA, but also as it means I finally have a depository for all the nuggets of Sussex's past that I've never found a truly happy home for before (such as that mackerel was once used by Brighton fisherman as currency or that Sussex once employed a 'County Organiser of Beekeeping'). It's also led me to investigate new areas to me, such as Sussex fishing stocks and discovering that Petworth House once had its own brewery. In the process of research I even found out that the animated children's film *Cloudy With A Chance of Meatballs*, where food rains down on a town, actually had happened in Kentucky in 1876 (it was believed to be meat buzzards vomited out in large numbers – nice!). I've not yet been able to discover what 'queer soup' was back in 1944, though, which appeared on HMS Lizard's Christmas menu (trust me, the Google searches were an experience!). This is also an exciting topic as even the words to do with food and drink in Sussex's past provide a glimpse into another world and demonstrate that food, in the

Above left: Brighton Blue. (Courtesy of Upper Weald Dairy)

Above right: Harveys Brewery, 'Cathedral of Lewes' and epicentre of the brewing trade in Sussex.

Petworth House – one-time home to a small brewery.

Special Menu for Xmas Day, 1944

BREAKFAST

0700—0730   0730—0800

Shredded Wheat
Bacon and Egg
Marmalade
Coffee

DINNER

1130—1215   1215—1300

Giblet Soup
Roast Turkey
Stuffing
Sausages
Boiled Ham
Brussel Sprouts
Roast Potatoes
Xmas Pudding
Rum Sauce

USUAL CHRISTMAS FARE
IF AVAILABLE

TEA

Fruit Cake

Swiss Rolls

Butter

Jam

SUPPER

Queer Soup
Cold Turkey
Cold Ham & Tongue
Mixed Pickles
Coffee

HMS Lizard's Christmas menu, with enclosed mystery of 'queer soup'. (Courtesy of RPAM BAH)

days before freezing and refrigeration and with the ever-present threat of bad harvests, mattered much to Sussex folk. For example, a Littlehampton dish once existed called a 'Swimmer', which was where a poor family had a bowl of gravy with just one dumpling in it – the children had to fight for it. In the county's past the demon drink suggest that today's problems of over-indulgence and illness from excess imbibing are nothing new, just as is the good cheer spoken of, and the fondness for, a drop of the drink.

Like many things in history, food and drink shows us just how foreign a country previous centuries were. Even studying a few centuries back makes us realise how different language with regard to food. Just to prove this, let's have a game of 'Should You Scoff or Keep Well Off?' (In other words, how many of these things from Sussex's past *should* or *shouldn't* you eat?)[*]

1) Old January Butter
2) Devil's Children
3) A Dish of Tongues
4) Earl Thurlow's Egg
5) A Burned Baby's Arm
6) Thames Mud
7) Thimble Pie
8) Wheatears
9) The Sussex Orlotan
10) Mice
11) Winter Picks

Ready for more? If I've whet your appetite for things that you're not sure whether to eat or not, let's investigate some more. Firstly, 'Chinkerberry Rings': these sound inedible but were actually small scallops, named as such by Sussex fishermen because they were found directly offshore from the Downland peak of Chanctonbury Ring. Talking of the sea, 'coast' was nothing fish-related, but was the name for the ribs of an animal, particularly lamb. 'Cocks' were small fishing boats, nothing to do with anything bird-related or anything ruder. And correspondingly a 'cockheak' was a net from one of these boats. You'd think then that 'cockle' logically therefore meant the seafood these boats caught,

---

[*] **Answers: 1)** No – this is the old word for mud in Sussex. **2)** Could do – it means 'magpies'. **3)** Not possible – this is the old Sussex phrase for getting a telling off. **4)** Yes – Earl Thurlow was an owl who lived at Arundel Castle. **5 and 6)** Yes – these were nicknames for puddings in the past at Roedean School. **7)** No – this was a brutal-sounding punishment delivered by the headmistress at Thakeham School in the 1800s (it's very lovely now!). **8)** Yes – these were small birds Sussex shepherds used to trap and sell to London restaurants. Londoners would also venture to Brighton just to eat them. **9)** Yes – another name for Wheatears, which were so called because of their tails and not because they lived on wheat. **10)** Yes – that is, if you believed Sussex medical men of the past who prescribed eating them to treat whooping cough. **11)** Yes – this is an old name for sloe berries, which go well in gin and tonic.

Chanctonbury Ring, from where the small Sussex scallops called 'Chinkleberry Rings' took their name.

Brighton fishermen in the early 1860s. (Courtesy of RPAM BAH)

but it was actually a term for parboiling. 'Chizzle' meant bran and a 'chopper' was nothing to do with 1970s bikes or axes, but the name for a dried pig's face. Mmmmmmm!

Pig's head was also a favourite Norman Christmas dish. It wasn't just the head, most parts of the pig were eaten in Sussex up to the second half of the twentieth century. There was a Sussex dish called 'Pettitoes', which consisted of boiled meat from the trotters that was cut into finger-shaped portions, dipped in batter with parsley and fried in deep fat. This tended to be served for breakfast or as a post-theatre dish in the early 1900s, the early years of the car. Speaking of cars, it was possible to nibble on a 'clutch', but this was nothing to do with the workings of automobiles, rather it was Sussex lingo for a brood of chickens or a covey of partridges.

Moving on from savoury courses to desert, baking in Sussex could also be confusing as in the past the words 'biscuit' and 'cake' interchanged their usual meaning. Some sweet dishes had misleading names too. 'Blackeyed Susan' sounds like violence had taken place, but thankfully it was only a well pudding with plums or raisins in it – the name given to a Sussex Pond Pudding when altered this way. Conversely, a 'Bread-and-Cheese-Friend' sounds like a dish but it wasn't; it was a true friend (as distinguished from someone just after your food). It sounds like Sussex folk used to not so much eat their hats but their wigs instead as the phrase 'butter-my-wig' existed, but this was just a strong declaration you were against something: 'No I wunt; butter my wig if I will!'. 'Fill-dick' referred to February, bizarrely. Whereas 'Hard-dick' was a type of Sussex pudding made only of flour and water (as opposed to 'spotted dick') – 'dick' likely meaning 'dough' in this sense. 'Skim-dick', conversely, was a cheese made from skimmed milk. Equally confusing are 'petrified kidneys', which are not to be eaten at any cost: they're the local name for the cobblestones that appear in Sussex streets in old drainage ditches.

What about eating any of the following: 'butter-and-eggs', 'patterns-and-clogs', 'Milk Maids', 'shoes-and-stockings' or 'Granny's toenails'? They are all the name for a yellow Sussex-flowering plant called the bird's-foot trefoil, which releases small amounts of hydrogen cyanide so probably best not to. It also has a variant with orange parts in the flower that used to be called 'bacon and eggs'. Could you cook a 'cabbage'? Not possible in the old Sussex sense of the word for schoolboys, as it meant to copy your partner's work. Eat anything 'carroty'? Nope, that was something made of wood. Would you brunch on a 'bungalow'? You wouldn't need to nibble on someone's home as it was the Sussex name for a type of limpet that annoyed oyster fishermen, so it is technically possible. Would you imbibe a 'bumboo' to wash down your feast? It was a drink sold in the 1750s in East Hoathly that was made of brandy and beer – the effects were said to be regrettable.

Dishes involving Yorkshire pudding can't be claimed as a Sussex tradition, but 'Toad in the Hole' is also the name of a traditional Sussex (and in particular Lewes-based) pub game, not just a tasty dish. It is played in pubs such as the Trevor at Glynde and the Lewes Arms. Pub games have been a British tradition for many centuries, but Toad has faced a revival whereas other pub games such as skittles and shove ha'penny have declined. It is played in a similar style across the county, but here in Sussex it is seen as vital that the table the toads (metal coins or discs) should be flicked into should only have one hole. The tables it is played on may look similar, but they have two or more holes. A similar game has been witnessed played in Peru, but it uses small flat stones. Lewes takes its

The Trevor Arms, Glynde. One of the Lewes area pubs where you can play 'Toad'.

Toad seriously, with a table being a must in its pubs and there is a vibrant (and sometimes potentially violent!) league between the pubs in and around Lewes.

'Roly-poly' was also another food-named pub game. It was played at the long-closed George Inn, which was situated at the bottom of the High Street in Steyning until 1939. This was one of the names for parlour skittles or ninepins. The demi-ball-like object that you threw at the roly-poly pins was cut in half, so it was called the 'cheese'. The aim was to throw the cheese in such a way that it spun on its circular side and knocked out the queen roly-poly pin before your opponent.

Sussex is also an interesting choice for a book on food and drink as we not only produce it here widely (Sussex still being an agricultural county), but with major domestic and international tourist destinations here such as Hastings, Alfriston, Goodwood, Chichester and Brighton and Hove it means there is huge demand for it too. Brighton alone welcomes nearly 11 million tourists every year and so the county needs to be marvellous at catering for numerous people at one time – sometimes in one venue. Just to give you an idea of the scale of consumption, back in the 1990s Brighton's Grand Hotel alone served 190,000 meals in one year – 70,000 breakfasts comprising of 110,000 rashers of bacon and 30,000 slices of black pudding. The staff laid 2,000 tablecloths in one big event, along with 800 napkins, 7,180 pieces of cutlery and poured 1,400 glasses of wine. You can't make an omelette without breaking eggs, as the old phrase goes, and neither could Brighton serve up so many meals without a price. At the Grand alone 26,000 pieces of china were broken every year – and that was without any Greek weddings!

Rather than breaking, let us instead focus on making – making you hungry, that is. We start with an appetising tour of the alphabet to whet your whistle and make your tastebuds

Right: A poster advertising the Grand Hotel in its early days mentioning its 'high class cuisine' and 'elegant table d'hote room'.

Below: The Grand Hotel recently – much larger but still a grand venue for eating and drinking in Brighton.

tingle. First on our exploration of eating and investigation of imbibing is wonderful word of 'appleterre'. This was a Sussex word for an orchard and an 'applety' was an apple loft, where the fruit is kept. Should you have wanted some honey to go with your apples, you'll need to find a 'beeskep', which was a beehive. Perhaps some 'cojer' or 'coger' might do the trick to keep you well, as it was your lunch (ploughmen liked their 'coger-cake').

A number of Sussex's other food phrases seem to be about cider and beer (in my own Sussex village alone, cider was still being pressed in the 1930s). If you went 'catterning' or 'clemming' it meant to go round begging for apples and beer for a festival on St Catherine's Day or St Clement's Day. As you did, you needed to sing this song:

Cattern' and Clemen' be here, here, here
Give us your apples and give us your beer
One for Peter, Two for Paul
Three for him who made us all
Clemen' was a good man
Cattern' was his mother
Give us your best, and not your worst
And God will give your soul good rest.

There is a 'catternin' cake that accompanies this too.

Pigs have long been reared in the county and it is strange that the old Sussex name for the weakest in the litter sounds almost like the name synonymous with the idea of survival of the fittest: a 'darling', or 'dawlin'. This was also applied to an unhealthy child. To make your child healthy once more you might need to track down a 'deese', which was a place where herrings were dried. If fish are not your thing, then you might want a tasty 'dredge', which was a mixture of oats and barley. To increase the flavour of your dredge you could use a 'faggot'. A faggot is today the name of a lamb-based meatball by Dr Brains (I never thought that was a great name to associate with food) or of course a homophobic slur, but in centuries past it was a bunch of herbs hung from the kitchen ceiling, or any dish flavoured with them. It could also be a bundle of wood used for cooking. 'Hopping John' was responsible for another great Sussex dish – a breakfast in days done by, but it wasn't a man. It was a dish of skimmed milk with a little savoury broth poured hot onto bread.

Moving in our alphabetical adventure from land to sea, Sussex has a unique language used by our fishermen of yesteryear. 'Dunkirkers' were foreign, dangerous fishing or pirate sailing vessels. A 'hoggy' or 'hogboat' was a small Brighton fishing boat that could be hauled up the stony beach easily. A 'Dutch auction' meant that fish would be sold in the Dutch style – with a high price first, then reduced, rather than the other way around. If you were successful in bidding, then the auctioneer would shout that you 'has 'em!'. 'Dees' were fires that herring were smoked upon in Carlton Row, a fishing area on the East side Brighton's Old Steine (once a fishermen's working area) and 'bending in' was the benediction, a blessing local priests would make for the fishermen on their boats to wish them a safe journey and return.

Sussex in the past doesn't seem to have been too worried about precision when cooking or working, which is why some of our measurements sound wonderfully vague. Take, for

A replica of a 'hoggy', a Brighton fishing boat on display in Brighton Museum.

Fishing boats off the coast of Brighton, with the West Pier in the background. (Courtesy of RPAM BAH)

Brighton Beach, showing how the shallow slopes on the Sussex coast made them ideal for smugglers to bring goods ashore. (Courtesy of RPAM BAH)

example, a 'dollop', which was a clumsy, shapeless lump of anything tumbled about in the hands. It makes you wonder whether calling someone a great 'dollop' progressed from this term. In the past this term was slightly more precise, though, as it also meant a parcel of tea packed for smuggling that weighed from 6 to 16 pounds (best transported on dark nights when the moon didn't appear). Another precise measure was an 'anker', which was a measure of spirits, roughly 7 ½ gallons. A tub was simply half an anker. A 'dozzle' was simply a small quantity, but it could be given if needed in a 'dracly-minute' (immediately). If you were offered food and drink and you were trying to keep to a diet then you had to just ask for a 'snoule' – a small quantity of something. Therefore, if your dough hadn't been properly kneaded then you might find you got a snoule of 'slut's farthings' in your loaf – don't worry, these are only little hard particles of the bread mixture. Finally, a 'drib' is a very small quantity of anything.

Roedean School seems to have had its own mini-language of slang in the past, one example of which was 'Thames Mud', as mentioned earlier. It didn't entail a trip to London and getting wet, but instead was Roedean slang for a chocolate pudding. The gruesome sounding 'Burned Baby's Arm' was also another not particularly appetising-sounding pudding. My favourite food and drink phrase, though, must be the wonderful word 'Twankydillo'. It was never used at Roedean, however, and is in fact the name of an old Sussex drinking song.

Being a coastal county there is no way we could leave out the great British dish that made it to our shores courtesy of Western Sephardim Jews who escaped from the Spanish and Portuguese inquisitions. I refer, of course, to fish and chips. When studying in Hove as a schoolboy Winston Churchill lived above the fish and chip shop on the corner of Ship

Roedean School, home of a unique language of names for school dinner dishes.

Street – still serving today. It isn't just Tories that are linked with our great British dish. At the 1981 Labour Party Conference in Brighton, Labour titans Tony Benn and Dennis Healey were staying at the Old Ship and were battling it out for the post of deputy leader of the Labour Party. Benn lost. Healey offered him a drink to commiserate, but Benn apparently stormed out and had tea at the same fish and chip shop that Churchill had lived above. His defeat must have made him hungry, though, as he returned to the hotel for his supper.

Fish and chips are a great all-year-round staple, but in the past the time of year also had an impact on which ingredients were at hand and, apparently, also on the powers of the food for healing and other purposes. For example, a devout man was supposed to eat roast veal and gooseberry pudding on a Sunday, according to an old Sussex proverb. Another was that if you ate winkles in March it was as good as a good dollop of medicine. Food could also hurt rather than help. Oak Apple Day was held on 29 May and dated back to the days of Charles II. On this day, children who failed to wear an oak apple or oak leaf (called 'sporting the oak') were whipped on the back of their legs with stinging nettles.

Sussex folk didn't just use food words for other meanings making past language sound like an elaborate code, they also rarely said they were drunk in the past and had instead a generous vocabulary for words for intoxication. They were usually 'concerned in liquor' or 'had a little beer' (when they'd had lots). If you'd 'had half-a-pint otherwhile' then you were a continual drunkard and 'none the better for what you took' means you were much the worse. If you were 'noways tossicated' it meant you were helplessly drunk, and 'tight' meant drunk too. Sussex folk in villages even rarely admitted to going to the pub if asked; they were usually 'going up to the forge'.

Above: One of Brighton's many fish and chip shops, and destination for a hungry Labour leader at a party conference.

Left: Steyning Brewery workers. Not looking too 'noways tossicated'. (Courtesy of steyningmuseum.org.uk)

Sussex Food and Drink Over the Centuries

Archaeological digs all over the county have unearthed some weird, wonderful and funny finds. Digs at Whitehawk Hill, above Brighton, led to the discovery that Neolithic dwellers loved their meat, which is very different to the veggie- and vegan-mad city in the twenty-first century. Excavations also hinted that Brightonians of the late Stone Age were possibly cannibals due to cooked fragments of skull and, more frighteningly, that the hilltop dwellers seem to have thrown their dead bodies out with their rubbish.

The ancient Britons who lived here before the Romans invaded favoured pork as their favourite meat and cherished it as a gift from the gods, which may be why remains of boars (as the later equally pig-appreciating Saxons would refer to pigs) seem to dominate the animal remains found at temples such as that on Chanctonbury Ring. Andredsweald, the great forest dominating Sussex, was valued highly by ancient Britons for the numbers of pigs the forest could sustain. Even Saxon weaponry was decorated with a little bronze boar figure (one of these is in Brighton Museum) and their literature, such as *Beowulf*, speaks of these decorations. The Saxons would eat boar at the feast of Yule (20–21 December) and pork remained the principal Christmas meat right up to the twentieth century. Many die-hard Sussexians still saw turkey as an interloper even in the second half of the twentieth century.

Pigs, a Sussex Christmas dish until recently, are shown here as part of a food waste campaign during the Second World War in 1942. (Courtesy of RPAM BAH)

At the far east of the county, Hastings gets its name from the tribe of the Haestingas who were not willing to be subjugated by the rest of the Saxons who landed in Sussex in the fifth century CE. In the eighth and ninth centuries they weren't happy with potential Viking conquerors either, so when the Norsemen landed at the town in the ninth century the townsfolk planned a daybreak uprising. Unfortunately, a crowing cockerel awoke the Norsemen to the imminent attack. In revenge, the people of Hastings afterwards played a game called 'cock in the pot' every Shrove Tuesday until the nineteenth century, where sticks were thrown at an earthenware pot with a cockerel inside. Whoever broke the pot first won the cockerel to eat, presumably with a ringing headache.

One arrival to Saxon Sussex in the seventh century was more welcome than the later Vikings as, according to religious teachings, he taught the starving folk of Sussex how to fish. St Wilfred (*c.* 634 to *c.* 709) was a Northumberland noble intent on spreading Christianity among the South Saxons. Landing on the coast at Selsey, he established his cathedral at a site now under the waves, but the religious headquarters of Sussex would be this landing point until the Normans built their cathedral in Chichester. The historian Bede puts Wilfrid's ability to convert the South Saxons to Christian teachings down to his ability to teach them how to fish, compared with the lack of success of the Irish monk Dicull on this point. Bede also acknowledges that the drought that Sussex had experienced for three years before Wilfrid's arrival

Hastings, home of 'cock in the pot'. (Courtesy of RPAM BAH)

miraculously ended once he was there, which would have meant both farmers and fisherfolk perhaps felt indebted to him.

Food was also a priority for the invading Normans, themselves the ancestors of Vikings who had settled in Normandy two centuries before. Once William and his men had captured Pevensey and built a castle there, the Norman army marched to Hastings on 29 September, where they would fortify and then 'steal some food' (according to Sussex author E. V. Lucas). Only then would they march northwards to meet Harold in October. William evidently liked his food, as the Conqueror's Stone at Bulverhythe near Hastings claims that it is on this he supposedly had breakfast after his landing in Pevensey Bay. The Normans were, of course, successful at Senlac – believed today to be on the site on or near the abbey in the village of Battle. Descriptions of the battle site of Sussex's most famous battle claim that Harold rallied his forces at a 'hoary apple tree' and Sussex ale and cider may have contributed to the fall of Harold's forces as they were said to be somewhat hungover after a drinking spree the night before. With victory in battle came spoils of war and the (now deserted) medieval village of Perching, next to Edburton, north of the Downs above Shoreham, was the territory given to Tezelin, William the Conqueror's cook following the Norman Conquest.

The Normans continued to enjoy boar just as their Saxon predecessors had and they too appreciated our substantial forests at that time, which provided the acorns their black-and-white pigs enjoyed. As mentioned earlier, the Normans enjoyed pig's head for Christmas. This was served in Norman royal great halls on a great golden dish, surrounded by a wreath of rosemary while hymns were sung and musical instruments were played. This was copied by the ordinary folk of Sussex too rather than having beef, and turkey was of course a much later option for the Christmas spread. The Christmas pork joint was traditionally a hand of pork stuffed to the brim with sage and onion and generously roasted until the crisp crackling was a deep brown. Apple sauce, just as today, was essential, but Sussex folk also had 'drip pudding'. This was a savoury suet roly-poly, which would pick up the drips underneath the joint as it roasted, having been cooked and sliced first. Accompaniments included roast potatoes, sprouts, parsnips, gravy and pease pudding. This continued up to the time of the Tudors, with even Henry VIII and Elizabeth I enjoying slices of roasted boar's head. Should you wish to visit a pub that celebrates this tradition in Sussex today then you have the Boar's Head in either Horsham in the west of the county and Crowborough in the east.

In 1591 the court of Elizabeth I visited Cowdray in Midhurst for a feast outside of the Christmas holiday. Today it is a set of romantic ruins since its fire of 1593, but in the sixteenth century it had huge kitchens. Lord Montague of Cowdray provided for his regal visitors thirty oxen and 140 geese – and that was just for breakfast one day! The one surviving part of Cowdray that didn't burn down from the 'Cowdray Curse' was the Kitchen Tower, which can still be seen today. This is where Britain's top chef of the 1600s, Robert May, was employed. Not only the top chef for a leading aristocratic family, May also wrote one of the country's earliest cookbooks thirty years later, *The Accomplisht Cook*, which seems to describe the first ever description of chips or at least sautéed potatoes. He recommends it with balls of parmesan cheese, so our local dish of cheesy chips has an ancient pedigree. We have to wait for Dickens in his *A Tale of Two Cities* (1859) for more literary mentions of chips: they're described as 'husky chips of potatoes, fried with some reluctant drops of oil'. Chips, of course, always taste best in the open, and al fresco

A Tudor feast with no sign of any sautéed potatoes. (Courtesy of RPAM BAH)

food was enjoyed by the Elizabethans too. Picnicking features as a leisure activity in Tudor times and the oak tree on the village green at Northiam is where Elizabeth I is said to have lunched – not once but twice – on her way to Rye. She even had a banquet underneath it that was brought from the kitchen of the nearby timbered farmhouse of the Bishop family.

The grand banquets at stately homes were only possible with the efforts of the numerous farm labourers and fishermen who made up the vast majority of the county's workforce until the industrial era and Sussex's development as a tourist destination. Being a coastal county, our fishing past is significant. Brighton's wealth in its early days was from fishing. Payments of mackerel and herring were even used instead of currency in Brighton in the 1500s and 1600s. It seems it was Flemish immigrants in the thirteenth century who helped our fishing industry take off. Our fishermen were foisted elsewhere after the storms of the 1700s destroyed their homes beneath the cliffs of the town. They moved from the Steine to Carlton Hill and the streets of where Churchill Square now is – these were demolished in the slum clearances to the estates built from the 1930s.

A much later picnic than that experienced by Elizabeth I. This shows a picnic from the 1850s on the hills above Fulking. (Courtesy of RPAM BAH)

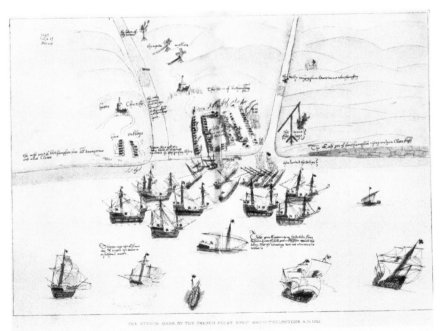

Brighton in the 1500s. (Courtesy of RPAM BAH)

THE ATTACK MADE BY THE FRENCH FLEET UPON BRIGHTHELMSTONE A.D. 1545.

Destruction of the Tudor town by the French. Note houses on the beach; the flaming beacons and the Militia coming to the defence from Lewes and Shoreham. Reproduced from 18th cent. engraving after the drawing in the British Museum.

Above: Fishermen and boats in 1860s Brighton. (Courtesy of RPAM BAH)

Left: Brighton fishermen. (Courtesy of RPAM BAH)

Above and below: Brigton Beach with fishing boats. (Courtesy of RPAM BAH)

Fishermen with their nets on Brighton Beach in the 1860s. (Courtesy of RPAM BAH)

Their workplace was also similarly shifted: well-to-do visitors demanded the poor fishermen off the Steine (it was a place used for drying nets and the smell of fish might have been one reason why the east side of the Steine developed later). They were moved in the 1880s from the fishing beach where Brighton Fishing Museum now is so it could be used for bathing; they ended up at the market in Circus Place, which eventually closed to them too. The last fishing families have since been berthed at the Marina. It's hard to believe the few boats left operating from the Marina now are the same industry that at one point in the 1580s employed eighty boats and had over 10,000 nets. It was the biggest fleet in the South, employing over 400 men who would also catch plaice, conger eels and cod. The fishermen still had a Sunday school for their children in the King's Road arches, opposite what is now the Waterfront Hotel, long after the fishing 'Lower Town' had been washed away by waves. Russell Street, behind the Brighton Centre and Grand today, is where the poor fishing slums once were. As a place with fishing in its blood, it is only right the industry continues today and its heritage is celebrated in the fantastic fishing museum on the seafront.

Brighton's private fishermen still take to the groynes and Marina today, which is only to be expected in a city with origins as a fishing town and that has sea creatures on its crest. There have been some unusual fishing stories over the years, many from the piers, which (like Worthing's pier today) locals had allowed to fish from them. The Noble Organisation banned fishing from the Palace Pier in 1984 when they purchased it, and the West Pier has been closed since 1975, so fishing today takes

Brighton Marina today.

Brighton Marina in the 1970s when it lacked the developments of today.

Brighton's West Pier in its heyday.

place off the arm of the Marina. Both piers in Brighton originally had landing stages that it was easier to fish from without attacking tourists with fishing lines as they cast off. Fishing was free on the Palace Pier until 1984 and for many years the town held weekly fishing competitions on the pier called 'Rod of the Week'. There is no record of any sharks ever being caught, although small ones were sighted off the Palace Pier in the 1930s. One keen angler was rumoured to be Madame Binney, the palm reader on the Palace Pier who apparently had a trapdoor under her stall on the pier from which she fished when clients were few and far between. For pier fishing today, the landing stage of Worthing's award-winning pier (Pier of the Year 2019) is possibly the most picturesque site in Sussex.

Some of Sussex's fishing traditions merit a return in the twenty-first century and would make great new cultural events in our food and drink calendar, especially with Sussex's St Wilfrid being so associated with fishing. 'Bendin in', the name given by Brighton fishermen for the benediction, should perhaps be the first proposal. It was the blessing that would be given at the end of the service to give protection and good luck to the fishing fleet about to launch to catch mackerel. This would be followed by a party on the fishing beaches (Brighton had two) called 'Bread and Cheese and Beer Days' given by the master of the fleet for wives, children and the fishing crews. This continued until 1896 and once the fleet had set sail and the mackerel nets were

Right: Mr J. J. David fishing from Brighton's Palace Pier in the 1940s when its fishing deck still existed. (Courtesy of RPAM BAH)

Below: Worthing Pier today.

Brighton women waiting for the fishing boats to return. (Courtesy of RPAM BAH)

The arrival of fishing smacks at Brighton. (Courtesy of RPAM BAH)

overboard, the fishing master would then say the following prayer, believed to have been written by the monks of the priory of St Bartholomew:

Watch, barrel! Watch! Mackerel for to catch.
White may they be like blossom on a tree.
God sends thousands, one, two, three.
Some by their heads and some by their tails.
God sends thousands and never fails.
There they goes then: God almighty
Send us a blessing it is to be hoped.

The return of the first mackerel fleets (usually by May Day) along this coast would also be celebrated with parties until as recently as the 1930s. At the east of the county in Rye the fisherman who caught the first mackerel would spit in its mouth to bring good luck for a large catch the following year.

It would be great fun to recreate these traditions and perhaps even to have a competition to see who can bring a catch in – from fishing net to fork – to produce the quickest Sussex Smokie, our local fish-based dish. With haddock, traditionally the main ingredient, being a deepwater North Sea fish it may be we could use a more local alternative, such as the mackerel. Further new Sussex food and drink challenges could include recreating a pub

Brighton market and the Town Hall in 1896 – on the site of what was once Bartholomews Priory. (Courtesy of RPAM BAH)

Rye, home of a unique fishing tradition.

crawl of eating and drinking in all of the pubs featured in Hilaire Belloc's *The Four Men* novel as part of a walking tour. Inclusions could be the Bridge Inn at Amberley or the Fountain Inn at Ashurst.

On the subject of competitiveness, Brighton may never have hosted the Olympics, but we did host two matches of the 2015 Rugby World Cup and also once hosted our very own odd 'food olympics' in 1820 when the prince regent became king on George III's death. The coronation poster advertised not just a '63-gun salute' but also a range of seemingly meat-themed events (perhaps a coded message as to Georgie Porgey's weight by this time). These included the 'chasing of pigs with a soaked tail' (to win the pig), 'climbing up a greasy pole' (to win some meat) and the drinking of pints of beer, aptly in ten hogsheads. Food included the 'cutting up of an oxen' for distribution to all. The music to accompany this meat marathon was very aptly, 'Roast Beef of Old England'.

Competitiveness over the size and quality of food has also taken place in Sussex's past. As a coastal county, you'd expect some fish of huge proportions to turn up from time to time from our seas. Yet it is inland in ponds and rivers that some of the most gigantic fish have been found. Back in November 1692 a trout was found in the Poyningswish pond at Twineham that was 29 inches long. A few years later in 1709 another trout caught inland weighed in at 11 and half pounds that was 3 foot 2 inches long. This is nowhere near the size of the gargantuan trout caught during the years that George IV holidayed in Brighton and that was given to Porky Prinny to consume. The trout weighed an incredible 22 lbs. Should you wish to believe that our longest river will give you the greatest chance of catching an equally long fish, then at 113 kilometres (70 miles) long, the River

Above: The Bridge Inn at Amberley – part of
The Four Men walking tour in Belloc's footsteps.

Right: George IV's coronation celebrations, complete
with food-focussed activities.

Medway is the longest river flowing through Sussex. Should you want the longest river entirely flowing through just Sussex for fishing, then you need the River Arun, which is 60 kilometres (37 miles) long.

Moving back from water to land, it wasn't just meat-focussed coronation competitions and fishing-based activities that took place on the Old Steine in Brighton. As far back as the Tudor age, Brighton was known for its black pigs that roamed the ground, which acted as Brighthelmstone's common land it seems. The pigs seemed to have been a noisy lot according to the son of Dr Richard Russell, who composed this poem in 1765 about their impact on the music played from the bandstand (where the war memorial is today):

> Those pigs' replied I grunting loud in the corn
> Round the Stand I suppose are to aid the French horn.
> Those pigs and those children are all trotting before us
> Assist with their squeaking to fill up the chorus.

Sussex may have claimed incorrectly to have introduced the first pippin apples, carps and the greengage to Britain but we did have once, at Bishopstone Tide Mills, William Catt, the grower of the best pears in the country in the mid-1800s. William Catt owned the land that was recognised as being the site of these pears. His knowledge of fine food wasn't just focussed on fruit as he advised no less than King Louis Philippe of France on how to mill his corn. Louis must have regarded Catt highly as when he was forced out of his country into exile in the 1848 Revolution, he made his way to Newhaven as a refugee and stayed at the now dilapidated Bridge Hotel, where Catt was the first to welcome him to Britain. Not far from Newhaven, a few decades later in 1870s Alfriston, Sussex held the record for a while for the biggest pear and the biggest apple ever grown. The village of Alfriston also gained national fame for the

Richard Russell's house, the Old Steine, prior to the 1820s. Russell's son composed a poem mentioning the Steine's pigs.

huge apple one of its cottagers grew. The fantastic fruit measured an unbelievable 15.5 inches across its circumference and weighed 11 lbs 7.5 oz. Traditional Sussex apple varieties still around today include Egremont Russet, Sussex Mother and Crawley Reinette.

Food and drink weren't just enjoyed in Sussex at harvest time. Our image of Victorian winters focus on the frost fairs on the frozen-over Thames, but Sussex also experienced our own mini-version of this, with accompanying warm wintery drinks. Hove's Wick Pond (now covered over by Lansdowne Place) is where Victorian skaters used to enjoy ice skating in the mini ice age of the 1840s, following a glass of hot spiced ale at the Wick Inn. Brighton and Hove hosted many exiles from the revolutions of the 1840s on the Continent and some lived near to the Wick Inn. One revolutionary who visited Sussex a generation after this inspired a drink named in his honour (and not just the famous biscuit): Garibaldi of Italy visited Susannah Stacey of East Chiltington in 1865 and she concocted the Garibaldi Liquer to celebrate her esteemed visitor.

Jugs of hot spiced ale would also be used by Sussex folk on Twelfth Night (5/6 January) when they were taken down to beehives so that the bees could be 'wassailed' with the blowing of horns, shouting and singing. Wassailing was the tradition of going around houses at Christmastime with a wassail bowl of drink in return for gifts – sadly, this was largely replaced with Christmas carolling. It also took place in orchards with established and new trees being blessed, but it was Sussex that extended the tradition to bless the bees too. The vicar of Amberley recorded the following bee-blessing song in the eighteenth century, which also talks of the fields:

Bees, oh bees of Paradise.
Does the work of Jesus Christ,
Does the work that no man can.
God made man and man made money.
God made bees and bees made honey.
God made great men to plough and to sow,
And God made little boys to tend the rooks and crows.
Blow the horn!

If you too would like to try the benefits of a wassail bowl, then follow the recipe below from Anita Lewis from www.sussextraditions.org.

To Prepare the Wassail Bowl
Simmer a small quantity of the following spices in a teacupful of water: cardamoms, cloves, nutmeg, mace, ginger, cinnamon and coriander. When done, put the spice into two, four or six bottles of port, sherry or Madeira, with one pound and a half of fine loaf sugar – that's the four bottles – and set all on the fire in a clean, bright saucepan. Meanwhile, have the yolks of twelve and the whites of six eggs well whisked up in it, and when the spiced and sugared wine is a little warm take out one teacupful, and so on for three or four cups. After which, when it boils, add the whole of the remainder, pouring it in gradually and stirring briskly all the time so as to froth it up. The moment a fine froth is obtained, toss in twelve fine soft roasted apples and send it up hot.

Now, the spices for each bottle of wine is ten grains of mace, forty-six grains of cloves, thirty-seven grains of cardamoms, twenty-eight grains of cinnamon, twelve grains of nutmeg, forty-eight grains of ginger and forty-nine grains of coriander seeds.

And to sing a wassail, then you'll need the words supplied by Bob Lewis of Sussex Traditions (to be sung to a tune similar to God Rest Ye Merry Gentlemen):

Sussex Wassail
A wassail, a wassail, a wassail we begin
With sugar plums and cinnamon and other spices in.
With a wassail, a wassail, a jolly wassail,
And may joy come to you and to our wassail.

Oh, master and mistress, as you sit by the fire
Consider us poor wassail boys who travel through the mire.
Oh, master and mistress, if you be but willing,
Come send us out your eldest son with sixpence or a shilling.

Oh, master and mistress, if thus it should you please
Come send us out your white loaf, likewise your Christmas cheese.
Oh, master and mistress, if you will so incline,
Come send us out some roast beef, likewise your Christmas chine.

If you've any maids within your house, as I suppose you've none,
They'd not let us stand a-wassailing so long on this cold stone.
We've wassailed all this day long, but nothing could we find,
But an owl in an ivy bush and her we left behind.

We'll cut a toast all round the loaf and set it by the fire,
We'll wassail bees and apple trees unto your heart's desire.
Our purses they are empty, our purses they are thin,
They lack a little silver to line them well within.

Hang out your silver tankard upon a golden spear,
We'll come no more a-wassailing until another year.

Speaking of the demon drink, back in the 1880s Brighton College kindly allowed hampers to occasionally be sent from home but stated firmly that 'They must not contain wine'. Allowing alcohol wasn't a problem it seems in the college's earliest years, as from 1845 until the 1870s boys were allowed a pint with lunch and another with dinner. This was halved in 1876 and ended up in 1885 applying only to the senior boys, but it might explain the two-hour lunchbreaks at this time! Beer, of course, at this time was drunk by children as it had purified, whereas water and milk were still often seen as dangerous.

Brighton College. Early college boys were allowed a pint and a half of beer with meals each day.

A reminder of the 1893 typhoid outbreak in Worthing is probably not the thing you want to think about when considering an eating place today, but one restaurant in Worthing has an interesting past. Mary Pacy, who was eleven years old when she died in June 1893, lived where today's Liming restaurant is. Its Victorian-era nickname doesn't help one's appetite either, being known as Pacy's Bloodhole. Her father, George Pacy, was not a contract killer, but he did run the New Street Inn and brewery – Liming Mexican Grill today. The pub, which opened as a simple beerhouse by 1845, had become a brewery by the 1860s when run by the Carter family. It gained its nickname from 1890s landlord George's tolerance of the town's fishermen gutting their fish in his bar. Had May stayed in her father's pub, despite its gory name, she would have survived the outbreak of enteric fever (as typhoid was also known) as the brewery had its own artisan well and her father had been supplying Worthing citizens with uncontaminated water. She had decided, however, to visit her friend in Broadwater, near to the new water tower, which gives Tower Road in the town its name. The tower was the source of the outbreak, and as Mary drank her friend's tap water she became one of the 188 casualties it is estimated were caused by the outbreak. Liming is a lively and charming restaurant today, and the location of many other nearby Worthing eateries such as Food, Montague's Tex-Mex and Tito's Spanish Tapas and Wine Bar. All of these great restaurants are a galaxy away from

Temporary water provision during the Worthing typhoid epidemic of 1893. (Courtesy of West Sussex County Council Library Service, westsussexpast.org.uk)

IMPORTANT!

All Drinking Water **MUST** still be BOILED.

Water supplied to the Tanks is NOT intended to be used for Horses and Cattle, but for Drinking and Cooking purposes only.

CHARLES C. COOK,
Chairman Sanitary Committee.

August 24th, 1893.

An 1893 poster of Worthing's typhoid epidemic. (West Sussex County Council Library Service www. westsussexpast.org.uk)

the dark days of 1893 when a town lay dying and Worthing became, to some extent, a ghost town as visitors stayed away.

Adopted Sussex polymath Hilaire Belloc first came to prominence in the 1890s as an author of children's verse and his career would last until the 1940s. As well as a reporter, politician and writer of many genres, Belloc was passionate about good Sussex ale, wine and food. It dominated much of his writing and sayings, ranging from the 'West Sussex Drinking Song' to discussions of the county's finest beers in his Sussex 'road trip' novel *The Four Men: A Farrago*.

Food and drink has also inspired the names of Sussex aircraft that were designed to protect and serve the nation. In the First World War, Middleton Seaplane Works built an aircraft known as the 'Bognor Bloater'. The plane acquired its nickname as it apparently had an unusual skin covering resembling the scales of a fish. Ten of these seaplanes were made by White & Thompson Ltd in 1915. They were officially called NT3 but were only ever known by their nickname. The RAF has, unsurprisingly, never brought the name 'Bloater' back into use, unlike the name 'Typhoon'. Despite its name, the Bloater was a rather slim aeroplane, probably inspired by the bloater fish, which has a similar shape to the plane's fuselage until they are bloated in cooking. The unique monocoque construction of its fuselage, where its copper and mahogany materials were covered in a skin, would have looked like it had scales and when varnished it would have looked shiny like fish skin – hence the name. The Norman Thompson factory, as the Middleton works became known, was not only one of the first of its kind in the country, but was the first to build flying boats according to West Sussex County Council and so we should celebrate these fantastic fish-inspired flying factory workers.

The county's biggest seafront hotel – Brighton's Metropole, as you would expect – gives us many insights into the eating and drinking habits of the rich and famous. The Metropole's Christmas 1944 menu gives us an idea of wartime food and drink, when the hotel was closed to the public for the duration of the war and serving as offices and accommodation as part of 'RAF Brighton'. Churchill made a secret visit to the town during

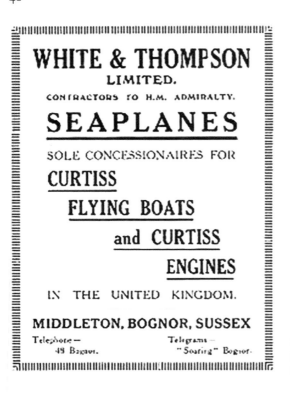

Middleton Aircraft Works advertisement from 1915 – home of Sussex's fishy-named wartime aircraft.

the war and three years later in peacetime. His stay at the Metropole in 1947, when he received the freedom of the town, gives us an idea of his dietary habits. It also perhaps also what he had enjoyed when a schoolboy being educated in Brighton and Hove. During this stay his wife, Clemmie, was said to have done most of the talking to staff, but the war leader did make the demand that his porridge only be made from the cream at the top of the milk.

Customers have always been demanding and the pressures on producers can be immense. One of Worthing's tomato growers back in the 1950s faced a rather wet death. The 1950s were when Worthing was awash with glasshouses growing cucumbers and Worthing tomatoes, which were famed around the country. The glum greenhouse man ended his days by drowning himself in a water tank as he feared his latest crop of tomatoes would be a poor one.

By the 1950s we get an idea of the poor state of British cuisine by the state of Brighton's biggest and most exclusive hotel, the Metropole. The hotel was not only losing money, but its food was 'terrible', according to Harold Poster, whose AVP Group bought the hotel from Gordon Hotels, who had built the hotel in 1890. Children today would agree, looking at menus from the hotel, which contained dishes out of fashion today such as ox tongue. Poster soon increased not only the number of kitchens and amount of food consumed with his 1960s hotel redevelopment and expansion, but also the different types and the amount of praise the hotel's food received. Not only did the new exhibition halls at the rear of the hotel (soon to be mostly redeveloped) provide new eating venues, but they had to provide high-quality food for more mouths than any other Brighton hotel. Rather than

GENERAL VIEW FROM THE SEA

Above: An unusual picture of Brighton's Metropole, temporary home to Winston Churchill in 1947 when being awarded freedom of the borough.

Right: The Metropole's 1944 Christmas menu, when the hotel was part of RAF Brighton.

ROYAL AIR FORCE   STATION — BRIGHTON

Christmas. 1944.

The Officer Commanding and Officers wish all personnel **A Merry Christmas and a Happy New Year.**

Menu

Tomato Soup

Roast Turkey   Roast Beef
Boiled Ham   Pork Sausages
Sage & Onion Stuffing   Gravy
Roast Potatoes   Creme Potatoes
Brussels Sprouts   Braised Parsnips
Cauliflower and White Sauce

Christmas Pudding
Brandy Sauce
Mince Pies

Cheese Biscuits   Cheese Straws

Apples   Oranges   Nuts
Ale   Minerals   Cigarettes

500 diners at a sitting, the hotel now could have over 5,000. The hard work paid off. In 1964, the hotel's Starlit Restaurant gained a feature in the coveted *Egon Ronay's Guide* and the highest rating in the town. This was reflected in how popular it was: Poster expected it to take £40,000 in its first year, but it took £70,000 instead. The new exhibition halls at the back of the Met (built over a decade before the Brighton Centre in a prophetic vision of how Brighton would come to rely on its conference trade) also encouraged new foods to be showcased in Brighton before anywhere else. For example, in 1962 the hotel hosted the nation's first ever 'Fast Food Fair', which may have been slightly more appetising than the veal and tongue that was on the Metropole's Christmas menu in the 1960s.

The Metropole, extended in the early 1960s to include Sussex Heights tower block and the Exhibition Brighton complex of buildings. This was a huge new eating venue for Brighton, supporting the conferences and exhibitions the town was attracting.

The Brighton Belle – focus of a fishy protest by Lord Olivier.

Brighton was the home of one of the most unusual protests ever in the early 1970s. Legendary actor Lord Laurence Olivier, who lived in the town and used the *Brighton Belle* train to commute to London for acting roles, started a huge protest when British Rail decided to stop serving his beloved kippers for breakfast. He was ultimately successful, but the trains were soon cancelled anyway so his efforts were unfortunately in vain. Lord Olivier's preferred breakfast may have disappeared but a most amazing one was rustled up at short notice and on a very grand scale just over a decade later. After the horrific IRA bombing of Brighton's Grand Hotel in October 1984, the Metropole (which was next door) took all the guests in and managed to serve them, the emergency services and the press an incredible extra 2,000 breakfasts that morning. Smoke-blackened and shaken visitors to the town were found clothes, towels and razor blades, as some of them had lost their clothes and toiletries in the blast.

Brighton's conference zone is due to move to Black Rock, along with the closure of the majority of the Metropole's exhibition halls and the neighbouring Brighton Centre. Black Rock was also the site of a bizarre 1970s eating experience. A number of construction workers from the Brighton Marina development were all taken to hospital one day in the 1970s when the artificial harbour was being built. The workers had been cheekily fishing for oysters that had been introduced to the sea within the concrete caissons that made up the harbour

The Grand Hotel just after the IRA bombing of 1984 – guests had to decamp next door to the Metropole for their breakfast.

Brighton Marina under construction. Its concrete walls would be home to a tricky treat for the builders of the artificial harbour.

walls (pictured) and had eaten a number of the fishy delicacies. Little were they to know that the marine biologists helping introduce the oysters and other sea life to their new watery environment had injected them with mercury. This was harmless to the oysters and was designed to help their immunity in their new home, but it was poisonous to the construction workers who were putting the Marina together. This was one fishy snack that hit back!

Overall, the post-war period was not the finest era for Sussex food and beer, though there is one exception. Banoffee pie was first created in 1972 at the Hungry Monk in Jevington by Sussex chef Ian Dowding. Inspired by an American recipe called 'Blum's Coffee Toffee Pie', the dish is now enjoyed all over the world. Dowding took the American dish and added between the toffee and the cream a layer of sliced banana to make the now famous desert. That wasn't all though. The American dish involved a difficult process of creating the toffee by boiling the mix of sugar, butter and cream, but Dowding involved his sister who recommended the trick of boiling tins of condensed milk, so the end result was both a family effort and a Sussex success.

In more recent times, food has played an increasingly important role in Sussex life, and also in the lighter side of things. Pattisons restaurant in Lewes at Christmas 1988 offered a cold porridge eating competition, and jeweller John Clarke offered a real pearl necklace to the first person who correctly guessed which oyster in his display contained the treasure. Sticking with sweet foodstuffs, boys at a school in Worthing in the 2000s were offered a 'custard-breathing' competition. This involved seeing how long boys could stick their heads in a bowl of custard for without breathing.

From the twentieth to the twenty-first century, Sussex is leading the way in food innovations even deep in our Downland countryside. As a pretty Downland village east of Lewes, Firle is known for fantastic views, its perfect pub, village walks and busy brewery, not for its fast-food outlets. So, when the news broke in the *Argus* in January 2017 that the village was to get a drive-through it initially raised eyebrows. Had McDonald's or suchlike expanded their empire to deepest darkest Sussex? Were villages now being threatened with cartons of fries and mess from milkshakes? Thankfully, no. Being one of Sussex's gems, Firle's drive-through would be for one day only. It would be for specially invited guests and would serve Michelin-star food courtesy of award-winning chef Simon Rogan. Rogan's plans were that Firle was to be the blueprint for Michelin-starred drive-throughs across the country. Rather than cars queuing around a burger emporium, the lucky guests were given a Range Rover for the weekend to explore the village, which they then queued in for exquisite food served from a luxurious drive-through. Simon, the owner

Firle, home to the country's poshest drive-through – Sussex-style. Perhaps more correctly, using the county's motto, a 'We wunt be druv-through'?

of L'Enclume located in Cartmel, Cumbria, currently holds two Michelin stars and his farm (which supplies more than 90 per cent of his produce) grows a range of unusual and exciting ingredients such as Japanese wineberries, elkhorn fern and buck's-horn plantain. L'Enclume was named the number one restaurant in the UK in the 2017 *Good Food Guide* for the fourth year running, with the restaurant awarded a perfect ten cooking score. With the country's first five-star drive-through, Sussex should be proud of foodie Firle.

On the subject of fast-food, Radio 2 reported in March 2017 of the story of a Peacehaven woman who managed to make the incredible journey from her home to Hove where she was attending a dinner party. Responsible for taking the sweet course, she had opted for a cheesecake and put it on top of her car as she loaded her other possessions inside. Unfortunately, she then forgot to take the cheesecake off the roof of her car, but the tasty desert managed to remain on top of her vehicle all the way along the A259, arriving safely 40 minutes later. The faces of drivers and pedestrians passing or overtaking the desert driver must have been priceless – perhaps the grin it gave many people was, like the cake, a bit cheesy?

Finally, speaking of cheese, not only can you eat the delicious dairy product in Sussex, but you can stay inside it! Hastings is home to the bright yellow Piece of Cheese Cottage, which claims to be the only residence in the nation with three sides. The cottage, which is in Hastings Old Town, also claims to be the second smallest in Britain and was apparently built for a £5 bet in 1871. It was up for sale at the time of writing and at considerably more than £5. We shall now look at other Sussex foodie locations.

A piece of cheese you can't eat! The unique B&B in Hastings is named the Piece of Cheese due to its unusual wedge shape.

Exterior view of the Piece of Cheese.

Foodie Places

Before looking at the stately homes, royal kitchens, rivers, fields and farmhouse kitchens that throughout the centuries have made Sussex the foremost food destination it is today, we must start with the most extravagant of our dining rooms – George IV's Royal Pavilion. Known not just for his love of women but also of food, George managed to combine the two once in this room when he paused from chasing a servant girl he fancied around the Pavilion to eat a chunk of pastry-covered game pie. His friend the libertine Beau Brummell remarked, 'I hope that I am never that damned hungry!' To which George replied, 'You will be' in between mouthfuls, 'but that may be afterwards.' He was also once asked at a drunken dinner party how many wives he had by the Duke of Greevey, to which George promptly replied, 'You mean apart from my own?'

Let's start our tour in the west of the county. The western River Rother, which flows into the Arun, is the only location in Sussex where native white clawed crayfish can be found. It is a truly fertile river when it comes to edible fish. The upper reaches of the Rother are important for the fish populations of brown trout, grayling, juvenile sea trout and the spawning and early development of salmonids. You can also find populations of eel, bullhead lamprey (famously believed to have been responsible for the death of Henry I) minnows and stone loach. You can also find bream, pike, roach, chubb (once also the surname of a Hove headteacher), dace and perch on the lowest reaches. Chichester Canal is no less teeming with fish. You can find roach, rudd, perch, common, crucian and mirror carp, bream, tench, pike, eels and then, if that doesn't make you happy, some dace and chubb.

The Royal Pavilion. Location of much hilarity and hijinks during banquets held by George IV.

Above: The Spread
Eagle hotel in
Midhurst – site of a
unique Christmas
food tradition.

Right: The Spread
Eagle, Midhurst.

Visitors to the Spread Eagle in Midhurst, dating back to the fifteenth century, can get to experience a unique Christmas tradition: Christmas puddings get stuck up to the ceiling of its dining room every Boxing Day. Another visitor to Sussex back in 1805 would also have enjoyed our Christmas traditions here today, in a foodie location in Worthing. Visitors to the Pizza Express Worthing outlet tucked away in Stanford Square may not realise that they are chomping on a calzone or gobbling garlic bread in the place where Jane Austen once lived, possibly for as long as several months between the autumn of 1805 and into 1806. Stanford's Cottage, as it once was back in 1805, had lavish views sweeping down to the sea (today the Stagecoach bus garage is unfortunately in the way) and was the home of Mr Stanford, a piano dealer, who let out his property to Jane Austen and her family. Hungry visitors to Pizza Express therefore get a literary bonus to any meal at the restaurant, as they are staying where one of the country's greatest writers lived. The one-time Stanford's Cottage will remain a Mecca for Austenites worldwide. There is no fear that the building will revert to its former occupation as a fruit and vegetable store, which unbelievably it was for nearly a century.

The Jury's Inn Waterfront hotel in Brighton (originally the Ramada Renaissance and at one point called the Thistle Hotel) is one of our most accommodating foodie venues. In the 1980s when the hotel first opened late Status Quo guitarist Rick Parfitt (who sadly died in 2016) stayed at the hotel after a concert and was allowed to do all his own cooking in the hotel's kitchens.

If you don't fancy doing your own cooking like Rick Parfitt did, there are of course the numerous options that you have when dining in one of Sussex's many pubs. One of the greatest novels ever written about Sussex, the very clever *The Four Men: A Farrago*, explores a number of these. The four characters in Belloc's 1911 opus eat and drink in the county's pubs from the George at Robertsbridge to their final destination north of Chichester. Many of these pubs are still around today, such as the George, the Fountain at Ashurst, the Frankland Arms in Washington and the White Horse in Storrington. You too can sup and dine in these, but it is recommended that you don't copy the scene from *The Four Men* when one of the four main characters, the Sailor, 'baptises' his co-traveller the Philosopher by pouring a tankard of ale over his head. *The Four Men* is a clever novel

Pizza Express, Worthing. Experience the location of Jane Austen's holiday home while munching on a margherita.

Jury's Inn Brighton Waterfront Hotel.
A mouthful to pronounce, but it once let a
famous guest cook his own food to maintain
the status quo.

as it works on so many levels: religious treatise, philosophical debate on the subject of being, discussions of the soul and mortality, a biography of Belloc, a work of adoration to Sussex (sometimes at the expense of Kent!) and, of course, a homage to Sussex food and drink. The greatest insult from the Sailor to another character, the more effete Poet, is when he insists that the Poet must be a vegetarian. The first character we meet (Myself) adds his criticism of 'water-drinkers also, and caterwauling outers, and turnip mumblers, enemies of beef, treasonable the immemorial ox and the traditions of our human kind!'

Belloc would have therefore applauded the sentiment of one dying man who we hear of through the contributions of Revd Howard J. Emmett, who regularly wrote for *Sussex County Magazine.* The man remained conscious as he approached the end and the reverend visited him to sit with him in his last hours. As he talked, he noticed the man's gaze swivel repeatedly to the ham on the sideboard. The sick man's wife came into the parlour where he lay and he said to her, 'I would like a bit oo that 'am; I would like it so much!' She ignored him and he asked again, only to be told, 'No, you can't have none of that 'am, we're saving it up for your funeral!'

The countryside, as reported once about Hurstpierpoint, was a place where you could find Sussex's wide range of natural ingredients that could be used in the past to treat ailments. Sussex hedgerows provided hedge mustard and could treat colds, asthma and horse voices; tansy ginger and lady's thistle were both stimulants to wake you up (presumably the latter if you sat on it); rest-harrow was mixed with vinegar to be gargled to cure toothache; melilot was for colic; and hart's tongue was for palpitations. If reading had made your eyes sore then you might want to pick some fumitory from Sussex fields, as it was good for sore eyes apparently.

Foodie People and Producers

Sussex has many people who have been – and still are – passionate about their produce. Midhurst's Cowdray House is where Robert May was employed – Britain's top chef in the 1600s. May wrote one of the country's earliest cookbooks, *The Accomplisht Cook*. Another stately home that merits a mention is Brightling Park, one-time home of John 'Mad Jack' Fuller, one of Sussex's most unusual MPs in the early nineteenth century. Fuller's speeches in the Commons were incredibly random and he once was suspended for calling the Speaker of the House 'an insignificant little fellow in a wig'. Fuller's other nickname was 'the Hippopotamus' in recognition of his 22-stone frame gained from huge banquets and heavy drinking. He was said to have been buried sat upright in a chair at a table, enjoying a final banquet in his pyramid-shaped tomb in Brightling churchyard. Sadly, this was proved to be apocryphal some years back. Despite being a true-blue Tory, he spent much of his wealth accumulated from his family's ironworks and slave trading on philanthropy, ensuring there was work for the local unemployed members of his estate so they avoided poverty and starvation. As the character Myself tells us in *The Four Men*, Fuller 'spent all his great fortune upon the poor of Sussex and

Cowdray House in Midhurst, where the kitchen of Robert May, England's top seventeenth-century chef, existed before Cowdray's disastrous fire.

of his own parish, bidding them drink deep and eat hearty as being the habits best preservative of life, until at last he died. There is the story of Fuller of Brightling, and may we all deserve as well as he'.

Belloc seems to have greatly appreciated the labouring classes of Sussex for making his beer and producing the cheese, eggs and bacon he loved. But Belloc seems even more in admiration of Fuller, whose belief in wealth sharing Belloc emulated, insisting that the four men in question pay for the ale of the labourers they meet and who serve them 'because we were better off than they'. This reflects his leftist leanings at this time (he had recently been a Liberal MP) and his exploration of what would later become known as 'distributionism'.

Sussex was also home to the workshop of the inventor of the machine that makes the world's most fantastic ever breakfast. This machine was the ingenious invention of Caracatus Potts, played by Dick Van Dyke in *Chitty-Chitty-Bang-Bang*. Operating since 1870, the East Chiltington Forge was chosen by Rowland Emett (a local artist, sculptor and illustrator) for the final stages of construction of the film's car and machinery used in the film. These included Potts's breakfast-making machine, which made 'sausage and eggs, mah favourite', as Grandpa Potts said, along with the gramophone from the 'hushaby mountain' scene and other props.

Sussex is well known for its huge range of culinary delights – both today and in the past. Perhaps the most unusual offering from our county must be one of our clergy, who not only produced a tasty dish for people from the Fiji Islands – he was it! Revd Thomas Baker, who hailed from Playden in Sussex, was eaten back in 1867 by tribesmen from Nivosa, which is on Viti Levu in Fiji, after making the fatal error of removing a comb from the chieftain's hair, although the Fijians were also rebelling against the encroach of Christianity at this time. The removal of the comb was apparently punishable by death by eating; however, back in 2003 the new chieftain issued a formal apology on behalf of his ancestors' behaviour. The museum in Fiji still has the soles of the reverend's sandals; they were boiled by the tribe, but, it seems, more unpalatable than the rest of the missionary.

Brighton isn't known for its cannibalism, but it is renown as being a city of vegans, vegetarians, organic health food fans and fair traders. It also has, along with other towns and cities, the ultimate in environmentally friendly food projects: the Real Junk Food Project. Located in Brighton, this is part of a global organic organisation that makes sure that food goes to bellies and not bins, intercepting food before it goes to landfill – hence the name. A church in Gloucester Place was the first outlet of this amazing organisation. This great project was set up in 2014 and caught the press's attention by having a 'pay as you feel' Friday café where diners were allowed to decide what their meal was worth and honestly pay their chosen amount. Director Adam Buckingham, who set up the project, now has a team of volunteers who provide over 350 meals a week out of food that would otherwise be making its way to landfill, despite being perfectly fine to eat. The project has spread across the city, with supermarkets, shops, restaurants and cash-and-carry wholesalers all providing food. Being Brighton the food is of course healthy, helping to ensure many a healthy waist rather than lots of unhealthy waste.

The first recorded pie recipe dates back to the Romans and consisted of a rather contemporary sounding rye crust, filled with goat's cheese and honey. Pies (or 'pyes' in Old English) first appeared around the twelfth century and usually contained meat, spiced with pepper and dried fruit. Sweet fruit pies make an appearance around the sixteenth century, although it is probably apocryphal that Elizabeth I made the first cherry pie. Sussex has its own pie in the form of the much-forgotten 'Churdle', which is not surprising considering its filling of chopped lamb's liver and bacon topped off with cheese. Believed to have originated around Chichester in the 1600s, its name originates from the old usage of 'churd', meaning 'to turn over'. This would have been a working man's lunch to go and, like the Cornish pasty of the tin miners of Cornwall, the purpose of the crust may have been as a handhold that could be discarded by the dirty workers' fingers that touched it. Pie making thankfully continues in Sussex due to Turner's Pies, whose award-winning pies are now found across West Sussex and have been baking since 1933. Higgidy Pies, who started producing in Shoreham back in 2003, can now be found in supermarkets across the country. The Sussex Pie Company have been running since 2012 and Newhaven's Tailor Made Bakery and the Real Pie Company are two other award-winning companies – the latter based in Crawley. My favourite pie shop, however, as a Brighton lad still remains Bangers in Baker Street, around the corner from where I grew up. I am biased, but their lamb and beano pies are a wonder of the modern world.

Another adopted Sussex foodie with a great appetite was of course George, the Prince of Wales, regent between 1811 and 1820 and George IV from 1820 to 1830. He was partly drawn to Brighton to cure the problems of the glands that Lewes physician Dr Richard

Bangers Pie Shop in Brighton, with some elderly customers waiting outside for pie.

Above: Interior of Bangers Pie Shop, Brighton.

Right: Richard Russell, the original 'Doctor Brighton', whose seawater cures led to the unique Brighton medical cocktail of milk and the briney.

Russell specialised in treating in his surgery on Brighton's Old Steine (today where the Royal Albion hotel is). Russell's portraits show a man clearly not too healthy himself in his later years through over-indulgence. His contribution to the development of Brighton cannot be questioned, but his addition to the canon of Sussex drinks certainly is. One of Russell's remedies was the prescription of milk mixed with seawater. It's no wonder the prince also overate, it was probably to get the taste out of his mouth. One of George's banquets at the Pavilion had 116 courses and were so rich and over-indulgent that they gave his younger brother, William IV, gout when he tried to eat them and his wife, Queen Adelaide, stomach pains. The Pavilion, unsurprisingly, was the centre of all things foodie at this time. George's head chef would sell off his exquisite dishes meant for the prince and his guests to locals from the side door of the Pavilion (particularly pâté apparently) and pocket the proceedings. The problem with that was that staff were meant to share any ill-gotten gains among themselves.

Perhaps 'Silly Billy' should have tried some of Russell's other prescribed treatments that patients would be persuaded to eat. These included woodlice, crabs' eyes, burnt sponge, cuttlefish bones, vipers' flesh and seawater. If you think these were bad, mice were, believe it or not, used in the remoter parts of the county as remedies in the days before pharmacies. It was recommended that you roasted and ate them and also crumbled them into a drink. This usage led to a mishearing by one Portslade mother. Her doctor had told her to put some ice in a bag and then hold it on the head of her poorly son, Tommy, to treat a malady. When the good doctor enquired a day later how Tommy was doing, his mum replied that he was feeling much better. 'But Doctor,' she said, 'I'm sorry to say the mice in the bag all died.'

The Royal Pavilion kitchen, where George's massive banquets were prepared. (Courtesy of RPAM BAH)

William, who succeeded George on the throne in 1830 and was himself succeeded by Victoria in 1837, had less-substantial banquets at the Pavilion, instead preferring less pomp, gluttony and bad behaviour than his brother's feasts, but they still needed cooks, waiters and local foodstuff. The king liked entertaining, 'Never was there a king so hospitable,' the exiled Princess Lieven noted. William tended to have around thirty people to dinner in Brighton each day and his way of inviting was an interesting one: he simply contacted the hotels and asked them to send him their guest lists so he could choose who to invite. William also dismissed his French chef, preferring the home comforts of more English food. Many of his naval pals from his days in the service were invited with the simple summons: 'Come along directly. Do not bother about clothes.' By this we assume he meant not to dress formally, rather than come naked, although in his brother's time the palace was incredibly overheated, to the complaint of many guests, so this option might have been desirable! The conversation was simple in William's day too, and Princess Lieven (who seemed to moan a lot) complained about the lack of politics discussed. After dinner, the queen would stich her embroidery while the king would snooze and apparently wake up occasionally to say 'Exactly so, Ma'am', as if he had been listening to the conversation.

Later that century one of the champions of Sussex food and drink was born. Hilaire Belloc, with his 'West Sussex Drinking Song' and his masterpiece *The Four Men: A Farrago*, celebrates the ale, port and food of the inns across Sussex. Belloc didn't stop there though, even writing a detailed set of instructions simply called 'Advice' on food, drink and its correct serving to his friend Bridget Herbert as a wedding present in 1935. It was published in 1960. He would also give friends and acquaintances meticulous advice

THE PAVILION. BRIGHTON

The Pavilion was also the holiday home to George IV's brother, William IV, who enjoyed less substantial banquets there than his brother. Note the unconvincing corrected misspelling of 'Pavilion' here.

A cheese plate of Sussex cheeses on display at Upperton Vineyard.

as to where to sit, when to arrive, how to address staff and what to order in various Sussex restaurants. Belloc's advice permeates through his writing too, especially *The Four Men*, which we mentioned earlier. The Poet, one of the characters in the book, makes the heinous error of suggesting they could eat 'some kind of cheese'. The response from his fellow traveller, Myself, is a stern rebuke where we see Belloc's love of simple Sussex fare:

> In Sussex, let me tell you, we have but one cheese, the name of which is CHEESE. It is One; and undivided, though divided into a thousand fragments, and unchanging, though changing in place and consumption. There is in Sussex no Cheese but Cheese, and it is the same true Cheese from the head of the Eastern Rother to Harting Hill, and from the sea-beach to that part of Surrey which we gat [*sic*] from the Marches with sword and bow. In colour it is yellow, which is the right colour of Cheese. It is neither young nor old. Its taste is that of cheese, and nothing more. A man may live upon it all the days of his life.

It makes you wonder whether Belloc would reconsider this today with our huge range of Sussex cheeses on offer, including Brighton Blue, the wonderfully mellow Duddleswell sheep milk cheese, Burwash Rose, Slipcote and Wealden Log, especially as one of our cheesemakers (High Weald Dairy) has even won prizes at the 30th World Cheese Awards in 2017–18. You would imagine he would approve of our cheeses being named after saints (George, Giles and Stephen) and the taking of Sussex cheddar and blending it with parmesan to create the award-winning Sussex Charmer. Both Kipling and Belloc, with their love for the Downs, would surely appreciate High Weald Dairy's latest: the Seven Sisters cheese – sheep milk cheese with a green Hebridean seaweed topping to recreate the famous cliffs. With his distrust of modernisation and 'the rich', he may have not liked the fact that High Weald's Sussex cheese Brighton Blue is provided by Virgin Atlantic on their international flights on their 'Upper Class cheeseboard menu'. Whatever Belloc would have thought, we should all be proud of High Weald Dairy's success (especially with it leading the way in sheep milk cheese) and the fact it is the home of the Sussex Cheese School, as well as all our other great Sussex cheese producers.

Today Sussex cheese is made from the milk of goats, sheep and of course cows, but an attempt to get milk in the past once highly amused George IV. Mrs Fitzherbert's ditzy, simple sister, Lady Haggerstone, once mistook her bull for a cow and tried to milk it. On the subject of non-alcoholic drinks, the Cokelers were a rare religious sect that was set up in 1850 in Loxwood by John Sirgood. They abstained from alcohol and were known for their drinking of hot cocoa instead, which is how they got their name. They didn't believe in marriage and so had no marriage service. Bizarrely, they refused to drink alcohol but were happy to brew it, so helping keep the Sussex cider industry going. The only reminder of them today is a Cokelers Close in Loxwood.

Above left: Ashdown Forester Plamin and oak-smoked cheese. (Courtesy of High Weald Dairy)

Above right: Brighton Blue cheese maturing. (Courtesy of High Weald Dairy)

Cheese turning – an important part of the cheesemaking process at High Weald Dairy.

A cheeseboard of High Weald's fine cheeses.

Cutting the curds at High Weald Dairy.

Above left: Yet more cheese. (Courtesy of High Weald Dairy)

Above right: Even more cheese. Wallace would approve. (Courtesy of High Weald Dairy)

Brilliant Breweries, Wonderful Watering Holes and Damn Fine Drinking Destinations

With one of the nation's most famous coastlines, quaint harbours and village pubs nestled under the Downs, it is no surprise Sussex has a wealth of wonderful watering holes and we explore these here – past and present. Sussex's chalky Downs also mean a purity of our water as it has been filtered by the chalk, and we also get water in places provided by Downland springs such as at Edburton.

Going from west to east (although in *The Four Men* Belloc does the opposite), we start north of Chichester at a pub that in the 1970s not only didn't serve food, but neither did it have electricity or toilets. Indeed, at the Royal Oak in Hooksway when you asked landlord Alfred Ainger where you went to visit the bathroom he would reply, 'I've got nine acres of field!' The recently reopened Black Horse pub in Amberley also had a similarly acerbic landlord in the last century. If you could drink three pints of the landlord's ferocious scrumpy he would give you the fourth for free. The only problem was that the cider was so strong that nobody made it to their fourth pint. Two, or two and a half, was the most people could handle. One local though, who was known for his thirst for fermented apples, managed it so frequently and qualified for so many free pints that the landlord had to amend his advert to 'drink three, get one free ... unless you're Cider Bob'.

A quick guide to a taster of the county's breweries. For West Sussex, you need to read Dr David Muggleton's excellent book *Brewing in West Sussex*. No longer independent, but still the biggest brewery in the west of the county, Dark Star began their journey to brewing dominance in the autumn of 1994 with Rob Jones's use of a one-barrel starter kit in Brighton's Evening Star pub in Surrey Street – not much bigger than a home-brewing kit. Rob named the brewery that led from the beers made from the starter kit after a song by the band the Grateful Dead, and so Dark Star brewery was born. He was soon joined by another home brewer, Mark Tranter. They relocated in July 2001 to Moonhill Farm, Ansty, and then as demand grew by January 2010 to the current location at Star Road Estate in Partridge Green. Mark Tranter broke away in 2013 to form Burning Sky of Firle in East Sussex, which is highly spoken of by none other than Miles Jenner, the chief brewer at Harvey's and so brewer-in-chief of Sussex, if there was such as title. Today Dark Star is owned by Fuller's, so Harvey's remains our largest independent brewery across the whole of the county.

Portslade Brewery may be no more, but the buildings are only seventy years newer than Harvey's Brewery (the 'Cathedral of Lewes') and are almost as fascinating. John Dudney founded a new brewery at Portslade, across from the current location, back in

Dark Star Brewery, the place where some of Sussex's most famous beers are produced.

1849. The High Street Brewery (as it was known) was constructed between 1881 and 1882 and supplied 'celebrated Southdown ales'. It was taken over by the Mews family of Brewers three years later who sold it briefly to the Kemp Town Brewery before another local brewers, Smithers & Sons Ltd, took it over in 1919. The building originally had a more ornamental sloping roof before increasing demand led to a water tank being installed instead on the upper floor. Smithers & Sons were taken over by Tamplin, and then Stanford & Sons brewed there until 1938 when they became bankrupt. The buildings then became a series of businesses, commencing with Shepherd's Industries and then Le Carbone from 1947, which ended up named Mersen until the firm pulled out. The decoration of hops, barley sheaves and the inscriptions 'D & S' and '1881' on the former brewery chimney still remind us today of its first incarnation as a brewery owned by Dudney & Sons.

As one of the country's major hotspots for hen nights, a centre of stag dos and an all-round party town, we cannot omit Brighton. Brighton has had numerous breweries in its history, no doubt helped by Flemish immigrants to the town who brought their country's beer-brewing expertise with them. Brighton's past breweries include Rock and Kemp Town Breweries, and it once had the country's biggest pub when the Metropole hosted the country's then biggest beer festival back in 1987. The Tamplins Brewery in Russell Street (demolished and now under the Churchill Square complex) existed for a fantastic 150 years until the 1960s. It started with one man selling beer from his house and ended up as part of a nationally known brewery. An old Brighton myth was that the place had a pub for every day of the year. That may have been true by the twentieth century, but earlier in 1889 Brighton had 774 pubs – one for every 130 residents, or at least

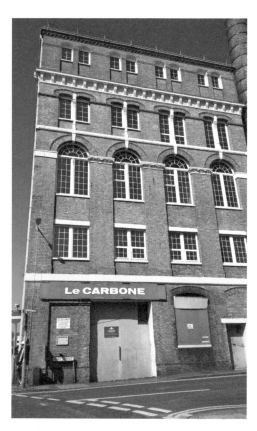

Left: The one-time home of Portslade Brewery.

Below: The decoration of hops, barley sheaves and the inscriptions 'D & S' and '1881' on the former Portslade brewery chimney.

The former Churchill Square, where the demolished Tamplins Brewery had been before the construction of the shopping centre in the 1960s.

two for every day of the year. A pub crawl of every pub in those days would have been very painful!

Sussex is known for its traditional ales such as Harvey's, but now our county is entering into the spirit world, with a movement into distilling of 'mother's ruin' – gin. Harvey's, our ancient and beloved Lewes brewery, has started distilling the tipple, probably as they have become fed up of being asked if they're the same company that makes Harvey's Bristol Cream sherry (if you look on their website, you'll see they are used to being asked that). But now, their response has changed to, 'no, that's not us, however we do make gin'. Head brewer Miles Jenner now has an additional challenge, as well as being responsible for a range of popular ales and stouts. Brighton is also a distilling hotspot, with Brighton Gin being launched, which means Sussex's biggest city also has a local gin to be proud of. It has also generated some truly inspirational cocktails, such as the 'Prospero', 'Brighton Delight' and, to celebrate the former photobombers of the West Pier, 'A Murmuration of Starlings'. Not content with that, Brighton Gin then asked friends to celebrate great British movies and so we have the delights now of 'The Theory of Every Gin', 'The Imitation Gin' and 'Gin Girl'. Should you want to make your own, then Newtimber Hill is one of the last places to find juniper bushes, which sadly once grew all along the downs.

Lewes, like many places in Sussex, is not just enjoying the craft beer revolution of recent years, but is also a traditional and much-lauded town of traditional brewing. Lewes once had nine breweries (and famously only seven churches) and while today the wider

Lewes area also has twenty-two microbreweries in the town itself Harvey's Best Bitter is still the default beer of many Lewes and Sussex drinkers. So dedicated are Sussex drinkers to the Lewes-based beer that there have even been protests when one Lewes pub dared to stop stocking the one-time county town's champion ale. So attached are (and were) the people of Lewes to their favourite brew, they launched a boycott of Suffolk-based Greene King brewery in 2008 when the large brewers bought the much-loved Lewes Arms and eventually took Harvey's off sale. The boycott of the Lewes Arms brought nationwide acclaim in newspapers such as *The Guardian* and *Daily Mail*, and it was featured on BBC News. The best quote was by the local Lib Dem MP at the time, Norman Baker, who said: 'This leaves a very bitter taste in the mouth, but sadly not that of Harveys.' The eventual successful victory by the Friends of Lewes Arms to restore Harvey's was finally achieved when Greene King's profits nosedived and they gave in, selling the pub to Fuller's a year later. This was not before 1,200 people had signed a petition and Harvey's jokingly had threatened to buy up Suffolk pubs and sell its Sussex ale there. Greene King's effigy had also been burnt at the Lewes Bonfire celebrations of that year and the Friends had introduced the inspirational idea of a 'disloyalty card': ex-Lewes Arms customers got a card stamped every time they bought a drink in alternative Lewes pubs and could total up how much money Green King had lost from their lack of loyalty.

The Lewes Arms today not only serves locally source food, it also uses food in one of its famous competitions. The pub is the home to some peculiar pastimes such as the Annual World Pea-Throwing Championship. The adult record is an amazing 38.7 metres, set by

The Lewes Arms, as featured on BBC 6 Music's *Radcliffe and Maconie* show due to its pea-throwing championship.

Danny Tear in 2003. The size, weight and outer skin of the peas are strictly invigilated. The event has regularly attracted TV crews from all over the world. It featured on the BBC's 6 Music radio station in August 2019 where presenter Mark Radcliffe explained how the contest started when the pub's barmaid Wendy split open a bag of frozen peas getting them out of the pub freezer. Regulars then started competing to see how far they could throw them down Castle Ditch Lane.

Competitions at the Lewes Arms don't stop there though, there are also marbles, pantomimes and spaniel racing! The best thing about the spaniel racing competition is that the participants don't have to be spaniels. Or even dogs. The requirements are the entrants have to be 'at least animals, who do not have to be spaniels but must dress like them'. Why not, indeed? The finest competition must be the annual 'Dwyle Flunking' match, which involves beer and is between the Lewes Arms regulars and the thespians of the Lewes Operatic Society. The contest dates back to the last century, or at least was resurrected around 1967 in East Anglia where it is called 'Dwyle Flonking'. The rules of the Sussex version of the game are apparently impenetrable, according to the pub and the result is always contested. Much Harvey's is drunk and spilled every year, but much fun is had by all, whether spectating or participating.

Harvey's was founded by John Harvey in 1790. Today producing 13 million pints a year, this makes the Lewes brewers the oldest but also the biggest independent brewers in the county. The beer may be brown, but the company is green: being local means barrels and bottles are recycled and even the by-products of the brewing process end up being used in local agriculture. It brews a champion ale too: in 2005 and 2006 Harvey's Best won the Best Bitter category at the CAMRA's Great British Beer Festival. It has recently been crowned champion in the Tourism Enterprise category of the Countryside Alliance Awards, held at the House of Lords. Unusually in this day and age it remains a long-surviving family business – the seventh and eighth generations of the Harvey family are still firmly at the helm. Harvey's is also special as brewery tours are conducted personally by the directors, late night shopping festivals are held in the yard and, quite wonderfully, the company has decided to let its dray horses ride through the town every week for no other reason than that they put a smile on peoples' faces.

Lewes also took an event that would have taken the smiles off locals' faces and commemorated it with a pub being built on the site. In 1836, eight people died in the nation's worst ever avalanche disaster after an overhanging excess of snow had built up over South Street in Cliffe. This occurred where the Snowdrop Inn now exists – its name now reminding us of the cold and crushing death these Lewesians faced in their homes next to the River Ouse. Lewes's river has also brought benefits to the town out of other disasters. When thirty people died of typhoid in the town in 1875 and the river water that Harvey's then used for their brewing was covered with a layer of scum, the chief brewer simply used it for brewing anyway. 'We used it in brewing', he recorded, 'purifying it by boiling, fermenting etc., turning out a pure beer.' I would have passed on that beer, personally ...

From one food and drink site with a much-loved castle to another. The railway by Bodiam Castle (a tourist destination in its own right today) was originally built not to bring visitors from Victorian days to the castle as Bramber's line once did, but was to bring hop-pickers instead. The hops grown at nearby Court Lodge Farm had as interesting

Above: Harveys dray horses.
(Photo by Paul Dearing, courtesy
of the Brewers Arms, Lewes)

Left: The River Ouse, Lewes –
source of inspiration for a
flood-focussed beer at the turn
of the century and source of
Harvey's beer during a Victorian
epidemic.

a journey as the hop-pickers, ending up with the Irish brewer of world-famous stout Guinness. Villagers who want a pint of the black stuff (or any other drink) also have a bit of a journey as the village's pub is not in the nearby village, but by the castle to pick up the trade from the many thousands of visitors every year to the National Trust property.

We mustn't forget the resurgence in Sussex wine since the 1980s too. Sussex wine is on the up, with our vineyards leading the vanguard of exports to twenty-seven countries. This has increased by a third from 2015 when Britain only exported its sparkling wine to nineteen countries. Sussex's lovely bubbly and wonderful white is now among wine from Britain exported to places such as Japan, Taiwan and the US. Our traditional wine importers to Britain, France and Italy now even take our wine. Wine from Wiston Estate vineyard was used to launch the P&O cruiseliner *Britannia* in 2015 at Southampton and to toast its first voyage. The Washington and Findon-based vineyard even owns an original Coquard press, of which there are only four outside of Champagne and theirs is the only one in the UK. Sussex is leading the way when it comes to producing wine, with a range of top vineyards including Ridgeview in Ditchling Common, Nyetimber in West Chiltington and Bolney Wine Estate. Ridgeview have said that their exports are 100 per cent up on this year compared to last year and export to fourteen countries alone. English wine producers have secured contracts with some of the world's most exclusive restaurants and hotels such as The Burj Al Arab in Dubai and the Ritz in London. Our chalky soil, warm weather and abundant south-facing slopes have made Sussex a wine-producing wonderland. And there are more vineyards on the way, such as on

 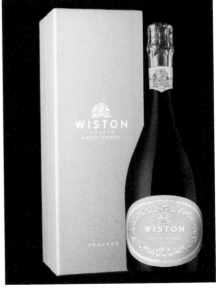

Above left: The very rare press at Wiston Brewery, North Farm, Washington. (Courtesy of Wiston Estate)

Above right: One of Wiston Estate's wines on display. (Courtesy of Wiston Estate)

Above: A Wiston Estate wine tour back in August 2017.

Left: Wiston Estate grapes. (Photo by Matthew J. Thomas, courtesy of Wiston Estate)

Wiston Estate in the sunshine. (Photo by Matthew J. Thomas, courtesy of Wiston Estate)

Sompting Estate where the first wines can be sampled from the mid-2020s. For history and vineyard tours of Sussex, contact Fizztory on 07504 863867.

Kirdford is worth a mention for the treatise 'The Degradation of Drunkenness', which appears on a plaque on a wall in the centre of the village:

> There is no sin that doth more disgrace God's image than drunkenness. It disguiseth a person and doth even unman him. Drunkenness maketh him have the throat of a fish, the belly of a swine and the head of an ass. Drunkenness is the shame of nature, the extinguisher of reason, the shipwreck of chastity and the murder of conscience. Drunkenness is hurtful to the body, the cup kills more than the cannon, it causes dropsies, catarrhs and apoplexies, it fills the eyed with fire, the legs with water and turns the body into a hospital.

Fine words, wonderfully written and all true. The only problem with them is that one story says they came from the vicar of Kirdford, who himself was a notorious drunkard. Another theory is that it was just one of several such temperance plaques produced in the mid-1800s, designed not so much as a warning to the drinkers in the pubs, but to brewers of home-made beer (which was often much stronger than that sold in the pubs). My favourite theory is that it was the villagers who had it put up as a public rollicking to their cleric. Whatever the origin of the plaque, Kirdfordians obviously haven't paid too much attention to it as the village still boasts two pubs today!

So, to keep the not-so-good reverend happy, we should finish the chapter with the purest of all Sussex drinks: Downland water. Sussex has been known for centuries for its medicinal properties of its seawater, but we also have chalybeate springs from where water bubbles up to the surface that were said to cure the sick. St Anne's Well Gardens in Hove was discovered to have a chalybeate spring whose mineral properties helped Brighton grow as a resort for health, and the other side of the Downs, Ditchling, also had one that was famed for helping Sussex folk fight rheumatism and other ills. The spring was famous in the 1800s but had gone out of fashion by the twentieth century. You can still see spring water emerging fresh from under the chalky Downs at Fulking by the wonderful Shepherd and Dog pub. The pub not only has served the odd pint of Harvey's, the Harvey's it has served also comes from a Sussex source. The Lewes brewery uses water from its own well, into which Sussex water has trickled through the chalky Downland over a period of around thirty years. Brighton's very own hidden river starts under the Downs at Patcham and is 'born' by a well (underground water) – hence its name the Wellesbourne. The water can be seen on the Brighton Sewers tour and it may be one day that a Brighton beer is brewed using it (hopefully before it gets in the sewers!). Ancient icy spring water trickles out from under the beach at Brighton that you can spot east of the Palace Pier. Not that you would necessarily drink it, but the Pells swimming pool in Lewes is also unusual as it is the only swimming pool in the county fed by spring water. It does have the effect of making one corner of the outdoor pool very cold, however.

St Anne's Well Gardens, where the chalybeate spring helped Brighton and Hove become a major destination for health-seekers.

Incredible Eating Places
Past and Present

From yummy Yeomen's pubs of yesterday to the grand dining rooms of royalty on visits to Brighton, here we explore the places to eat in the past and present.

One of the county's largest, grandest and most prestigious dining rooms that the public can still eat in today is the '1890' restaurant at the Hilton Brighton Metropole. When the hotel opened in 1890 it was the most exclusive of Brighton's places to dine, but also the largest. The 1890 is today the southern and sea-facing of the hotel's three dining rooms, but was referred to as the 'salle à manger' back in the hotel's opening year. This gives a clue as to the hotel's penchant for French cuisine as well as home-grown tastes from its earliest days up until the 1970s, with French cuisine seen as being the height of good taste. The three main eating areas were at first simply called the southern, middle and rear dining rooms and could seat 500 with glass partitions between the three. These dining areas continued along the entire eastern side of the hotel, with the front (southern) dining room being the most exclusive due to its sea view, and the north room facing onto the gardens. A minstrel gallery played music to entertain all three sets of diners. These rooms have faced many name changes over the years, with the south dining room (or 'Grand Salle') the most right up until recently when it even had two names, the Arundel (à la carte cuisine) and the Windsor (British-focussed food). It is today the Waterhouse Restaurant, with the restaurants behind it now the Sandringham and Ambassador conference suites. The 1890 retains the high ceiling and elaborate decoration it was originally blessed with by its architect, the prolific

The exterior of the Metropole today.

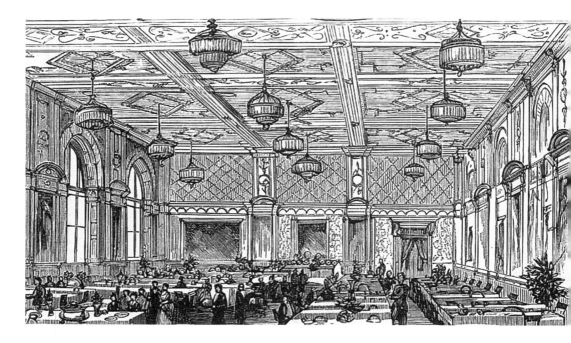

Above: The Metropole's
main dining room
in 1890.

Left: The Metropole's
Ambassador Room.

Alfred Waterhouse, and gives an idea while you dine of what the remainder of the ground
floor of Brighton's biggest hotel once looked like. Thankfully the Met is due to receive a
thoughtful restoration at time of writing, with the history of the hotel prominent in any
renovations, so hopefully we should soon see more of how the hotel looked back in its early
days when it was the most fashionable place in Brighton to dine.

Across the lobby from the 1890 is the Metropole or 'Waterhouse' bar – another place
to dine with great sea views in Brighton. The exclusive nature of the Metropole's dining
and drinking experience is revealed best in Patrick Hamilton's 1922 novel *The West Pier*

FINEST SEASIDE HOTEL IN EUROPE.

Cocktails at Brighton
Metropole's Winter
Gardens.

THE WINTER GARDEN, HÔTEL MÉTROPOLE, BRIGHTON.

when the heroine, Esther Downes, ponders whether which one of her two wealthy suitors, Gorse and Ryan, will be well dressed enough to be allowed into this hotel's bar to buy her cocktails. Twelve years later from Hamilton's novel, during the 1930s, the experiences of Metropole staff member Stan Vomberg were also illuminating as to the level of service during your dining experience: 'There were 24 waiters, no women,' he revealed in 1981, 'the waiters all wore frock coats, with white gloves on special occasions'.

FOOD-SHAPED PLACES

Some of Sussex's food and drink destinations even look like food, or they have been described using food and drink analogies. Firstly, Cissbury Ring has been described as being the shape of a jelly bean. The i360 has been described as a 'donut on a stick'. And the Pavilion was once described by Cobbett as being made with a 'large Norfolk turnip' with the green leaves cut off and with four other smaller turnips.

The Pavilion, once described
using vegetable terminology.

RESTAURANTS OF ROYALTY

Should you want to follow the Windsors, Mountbatten-Windsors, Saxe-Coburg Gothas, Hanoverians, Stuarts, Tudors and our other royal houses in their places of dining, then Sussex has plenty of options. Elizabeth I picnicked not once but twice at the tree on the village green at Northiam. She was on her way to Rye and her picnic was provided by the local Bishop family. She also visited Cowdray, where she definitely dined and apparently watched events in Midhurst from the window of the Spread Eagle hotel. Charles II, on his 'great escape' as Prince of Wales from the Battle of Worcester to exile in France apparently dined at the George & Dragon in Houghton, or at least supped a presumably much-needed ale. Despite the claims in Ainsley Harrison's book *Ovingdean Grange*, there is no evidence the fugitive prince stayed there, nor is there evidence of him staying over at St Mary's House in Bramber, especially as he was supposedly nearly caught on Bramber Bridge and so hurried along the causeway that then spanned the Adur. Charles did stay the night in the George Inn in West Street, Brighton (although some historians believe he overnighted in Middle Street), but considering he was a fugitive and Cromwell's troops were in hot pursuit, it is more likely he would have been on what was then the outskirts of the town – as near as possible to a waiting vessel for France.

George IV and William IV both dined at the Pavilion in Brighton of course, but William was said to be partial to the food (and other delights) at the (currently closed) Crown Hotel in Lewes. Edward VII helped Brighton gain increased status with his visits after Victoria's desertion of the town and visited the (still-running) English's Fish restaurant in Brighton's Lanes where the indomitable sisters who owned the restaurant back then told him off for lighting up a cigar. The Leigh-Jones family have incredibly run the restaurant since 1945. You can dine where many famous visitors have previously been, such as Charlie Chaplin, Lily Savage and Judy Dench. There is also apparently a ghostly gentleman in an oversized top hat that can sometimes be seen walking through their kitchens.

Moving west to Hove, the borough that was once separate from Brighton is always known for its modesty when compared with its brash neighbour, and this was even true with a cheese shop that only closed its doors in August 2019. La Cave à Fromage in Western Road, Hove, described itself on its website as 'the world's third most amazing cheese shop'.

King Edward VII, who was once told off in English's restaurant.

Roots of Today's Food and Drink

In recent years Sussex has seen a boom in new microbreweries, craft ales, spirits and food fusions. Here we investigate the cultural roots and historic inspiration behind many of these new food and drink names and recipes, such as the beer inspired by a shabby schoolboy.

Starting in the west of the county, Hammerpot Brewery in Poling was named after the nearby Sussex hamlet. In August 2005, the first two beers by Lee Mitchell and Frank Phillips, the chief brewers, were called Meteor and Red Hunter. The latter took an aeronautical theme, commemorating the Gloster Meteor and Hawker Hunter jets, which held the world air speed record just off of the Sussex coast in in 1946 and then again in 1953 respectively. Thankfully both aircraft made it back safely, unlike the ship that was wrecked off the Sussex coast and found to be carrying bottles of porter, in honour of which the brewers created the dark beer Bottle Wreck Porter, which was first brewed in 2007.

Greyhound Brewery in West Chiltington is one of the most interesting and intriguing new Sussex breweries, not least as it doesn't have a greyhound on its logo. The reason why it got its name was twofold: the owners, Nick and Sarah, once owned a beautiful AC Greyhound car, which they lovingly restored after forty years of being neglected in a garage. They even raced it at Goodwood. Italian friends of theirs also brought them a greyhound puppy and Nick owned a carved walking stick shaped like a greyhound's head. However, when Nick tried to make designs for beer logos with a greyhound's head on them, they stretched bizarrely on beer bottles and looked wrong. They ended up instead using a letter 'G' based on a neon sign from the garage and a yellow bird – hence the name of their first beer, Blonde Bird. Nick's greyhound walking stick had amber eyes and so their next beer, a golden ale, was named Amber Eyes. Today their beers are selling fast all around West Sussex – almost as fast as a greyhound!

A local beer by Beeding's Riverside Brewery, Dirty Arthur, is named after a Washington schoolboy who was caned by his school in 1895 for being covered in dirt. Arthur Adsett was from a large, poor rural family in the village of Washington and would go on to get even dirtier in the trenches of the Western Front. He died in 1916 at the Somme aged just twenty-eight. His name is the first that is remembered on the village war memorial. The PTA at St Mary's Primary School, Washington, back in 2017 decided to commemorate Arthur with a brown-coloured beer bottle and cap to mark the dirt he was covered in when at school, and when serving king and country. Riverside also celebrate dirt, or at least the dirt created from the smoke of the locomotive of the Shoreham to Horsham line that passed nearby until the 1960s where their Upper Beeding brewery is today, called the 'Steyning Stinker'.

The legacy of Maria Fitzherbert, George IV's secret wife, is the magnificent Steine House in Brighton and a royal love story. She is also commemorated in Mrs Fitzherbert's pub in New Road, which used to serve Jenga-style chips. Her influence was also felt on a

Left: Dirty Arthur beer, named after a Washington warrior.

Below: St Mary's Primary School, Washington, where Arthur Adsett was punished for being dirty back in 1895.

Brighton pub and an addition to our local language. The north side of Mrs Fitzherbert's house faces what is now the rear of the Royal Pavilion Tavern, which one owner – Edward Savage – decided to develop by opening a 'Gin Palace' at the rear, with a sign stating this wording. Mrs Fitzherbert took offence to the sign and apparently made the owner change it, so he put up a sign adverting 'Shades', either due to the shady nature of the passageway between the buildings, or to the characters who would be frequenting a gin palace. Mrs.

Steine House, which in its earlier guise was the home of Mrs Fitzherbert, who helped propagate a Sussex name for backstreet bars.

Fitzherbert was presumably happy and the word took off – a shades bar became Sussex lingo for a bar at the rear of a public house where the shadier customers would go. Worthing even had the Nelson Shades – a bar at the back of the Nelson Inn that was, for a while, Worthing's acting town hall.

As we journey east across Sussex, it is not just beer and buildings that have intriguing roots. High Weald Dairy's Seven Sisters cheeses resemble the famous cliffs, and Sister Sarah, their semi-soft goat cheese, is named after Sarah Hardy, who runs the dairy with her husband Mark.

Judges at the 2018 British Cheese Awards awarded Sister Sarah with a gold medal. High Weald's smoked Ashdown Forester cheese was also a winner, scooping a bronze medal for the High Weald Dairy. The awards, which took place at the Royal Bath and West Show in Somerset, saw cheeses from 147 cheesemakers judged, so this was no mean feat. Brother Michael is named after the man who was High Weald's chief cheesemaker for many years and the brains behind many of their cheeses. He helped the dairy's production facility move from Duddleswell in East Sussex to the current site in Horsted Keynes in West Sussex. It is hard not to be inspired by such a successful dairy. Sarah and Mark also offer tiered cheeses as an alternative to wedding cakes. And, most of all, they have admitted that they are so obsessed by cheese they have even named one of their dogs Pickle.

Continuing eastwards, Sussex's oldest brewer, Harvey's, has been always been celebrated most for its Sussex Best bitter. Its huge range of beers now matches Harvey's continued widespread success (it is now found north of the Thames). You can sup on a Harvey's stout, IPA or such intriguingly named brews such as Kiss and Tin Lizzy. Harvey's also brew Georgian Dragon which is a beer celebrating England's 'Father of Palaeontology'. In 1821, Lewes doctor

Above left: Mark and Sarah of High Weald Dairy.

Above right: High Weald's celebration 'cheese cake' for wedding couples who prefer a savoury wedding cake.

and fossil collector Gideon Mantell's understanding of fossilised iguanodon teeth (discovered in a Sussex quarry) heralded the start of the classification of prehistoric reptiles. It comes out on St George's Day every 23 April and is a pun on 'George and Dragon' (a common pub name) in case you hadn't noticed. Its artwork features Gideon Mantell's iguanadon, with a subtle red flag as a nod to St George's Day. For the romantics out there, Harvey's Kiss is launched for Valentine's Day every year and celebrates 'the returned kiss': in 2000 Rodin's statue *The Kiss* was returned to Lewes for an exhibition after having been resident in the Town Hall as it was rejected by the townsfolk some eighty years previously. Or you could have Sussex Nuptial Ale, brewed in honour of the marriage of the Duke and Duchess of Sussex in May 2018. Royalists could also sup on Elizabethan Ale, brewed originally for the coronation of Elizabeth II in 1953. This strong barley wine is reminiscent of the 'October Ales' that were brewed in domestic brewhouses during the sixteenth century. For literary Lewesians every June you need Copperwheat, which is named after the fictitious Lewes brewers in Mrs Dudeney's novel *Seed Pods* (1927).

Harvey's beers, many of which have meaningful and sometimes historic names.

Funny Food and Food Festivals, Eating Events Guide and Daft Drink Directory

FEATHERED-FRIENDLY FOOD FESTIVAL

Should you be a lover of our feathered friends and want a bird-themed 'food-crawl', then start by claiming the title of owner of Pevensey Castle. Whoever is the owner of the castle (the last was the Duke of Devonshire) is entitled to call themselves 'Dominius Aquilae', or Lord of the Eagle. After a picnic there, travel eastwards to Brighton where the Blackbird tea rooms won a number of awards, and then further east to the Hummingbird Restaurant at Shoreham Airport. If you stick by the shoreline, there is the Oystercatcher at Climping, or head inland for the more majestic Spread Eagle.

As well as Sussex's food and drink featuring in the county's history over the centuries, we must also remember that it features heavily in the county's calendar each year. So as well as foodie, beer, gin and fizz festivals you can visit, there are also holy days and other

Pevensey Castle, a site for a feathered-friends-focussed food crawl.

dates you can celebrate that would have involved celebrating using food and drink. Firstly, there was Birds Wedding Day, which was the old Sussex name for St Valentine's Day (14 February). Next, 'bind-days' were days when tenants of certain manors in Sussex had to work for their lord rather than their own work. For an example of the food they would need to typically provide for the lord of their manor, see the 'Bind Days in Bury' poem in the final chapter. Crouchmass was St Helena's Day on 18 August and, talking of ladies, Lady-tide was the festival around 25 March. At the end of the year was the festival of Goodening, when Sussex folk went around peoples' houses asking for aid on St Thomas's Day (21 December). This would help them provide for the costly forthcoming Christmas season. Slightly earlier was 'Waygoose' on (23 November), and there was a bean feast or celebration on St Clement's Day. During this festival Brighton folk would enjoy a roast leg of pork, boned and stuffed with sage and onions. Fill-dick was the most obscene-sounding date on the calendar, but only meant February in Sussex's past. 'Dick' usually meant 'dyke' in a number of old Sussex references, but in pudding terms meant 'dough'.

Belloc's birthday (27 July) has become Belloc Day – Sussex's very own version of Burns Night to some. 'Belloholics' (a phrase I prefer to 'Bellocians', as used by the Belloc Society) celebrate the life of the Sussex bard (as he should be known far more than Kipling!) by drinking fine local ale and eating the simple Sussex fare of bread, bacon and cheese that Belloc lived on. Belloc believed in 'the goodness of God in the drinking of ale, which is a kind of prayer,' and added, 'drinking good ale is a more renowned and glorious act than any other to which a man can lend himself'. Taking again to *The Four Men*, the best example of the four men in question enjoying a typical Belloc banquet is their visit to the Crabtree Inn in Lower Beeding.

Halloween is increasingly becoming associated with food, but for one Sussex producer they have undergone a journey starting with food and moving more and more towards Halloween. Tulleys Farm, near Crawley, in eighty years has gone from cows to making tens of thousands cower in fear every year. What was once a small dairy farm, bought by Bernard Beare from Devon in 1937, is today a huge Sussex business and destination for visitors from near or far seeking fun days out, farm produce and, most of all, fear. By 1991 the farm had tried producing salad vegetables and had expanded to have a huge 'pick-your-own' business. This was the year Bernard's grandson Stuart joined the family business and he was able to pick his own route to success. First opening a farm shop and tearoom, Stuart then decided to experiment with the booming US celebration of Halloween, which seemed to be creeping back to Britain. From growing just four pumpkins, the farm now has experienced a huge pumpkin festival, a spooky maze of maize and the annual Shocktoberfest. Details of their maze was broadcast live to over sixty countries in 1998 and the farm's Halloween events went on to beat both Alton Towers and Thorpe Park in 2008. The awards have kept coming for both frightening events and farm produce ever since. Not many places delight in both feeding and frightening us, but Tulleys Farm has achieved this for over 60,000 people per year and achieved worldwide recognition.

Finally, to celebrate Sussex all year round, our oldest brewer – Harvey's of Lewes – have a seasonal beer out every month. After quaffing their Christmas Ale well into January, you can celebrate the Six Nations with Forward's Choice or pucker up for a Kiss, which was launched on Valentine's Day. Each year March sees the release of Porter, which is brewed to the company's 1859 porter recipe. Olympia beer is sold in April and is linked to the Olympia Festival while Knots of May, launched for May Day each year, celebrates local morris men who dance from May onwards. Copperwheat in June celebrates Lewes's fictional brewing family of a 1920s novel, and Tom Paine ale was first released twenty-five years ago for 4 July – Paine helped inspire American independence. Lewes Castle Brown, out in August, is a pun on Newcastle Brown Ale and September is aptly celebrated with Southdown Harvest ale. As October 2004 was the first time Star of Eastbourne was brewed for the beer festival, it is still launched at that time every year, and Lewes couldn't celebrate its world-famous Bonfire Night without a beer, and Bonfire Boy does that well. Brewed with a smattering of black malt to give the hint of smoke, it was originally called Firecracker and was to commemorate the work of Lewes Fire Brigade who tackled the 1996 fire at the brewery. Not only has fire inspired new beers at the brewery, water has too. The 2000 flood that swept through the brewery inspired Ouse Booze in honour of the deluge that failed to sweep asunder Sussex's oldest brewer.

Harvey's deserves its own festival, but fans of Sussex's biggest-selling local brew can see the brewery every year at the Great British Beer Festival in Olympia and at Sussex's numerous other beer festivals. It is even now the case that cheese has its own Sussex festival. Unfortunately, its first year didn't go as well as hoped. The Big Cheese Festival in March 2018 promised cheese-themed music ('cheesy DJs and R and Brie') as well as 'craft beers, liquor and wine', but hit the national and international news after it ran out of … cheese. Headlines included 'Should have done Feta' (Sky News) and people took to Twitter, angry with the organisers for charging £22 a head for long queues, no cheese and few vendors, warning them to 'tread Caerphilly' in future.

UNUSUAL PLACES TO INVESTIGATE AND IMBIBE IN

With our hectic lifestyles we're used to eating on the move today, but here in Sussex you can eat in a classic form of transport as it chugs through the countryside. The Bluebell Railway regularly has meals you can eat on board its steam trains, and the Lavender Line at Isfield has an old Railway Buffet for you to eat in. Should these methods of transport be too land-based for you, then the Wey and Arun Canal offers meals as you navigate the restored canal in the north-west of the county. Coming back onto land, the Colonnade Bar in New Road, Brighton, provides a theatrical experience for you to sip cocktails or calmer drinks in among endless photos of actors who have graced the Theatre Royal over the years. You will also bump into the odd showbiz personality 'treading the boards' next door. Should the 'electric theatre' (as cinemas were once called) be your preference over actual theatre, then the Duke of York's Picturehouse has a unique balcony under its famous stripy legs, which can be hired for you to sip drinks as you look out over the bright lights of Brighton's Leicester Square, Preston Circus. If this is not odd enough for you, then the Jury's Inn hotel by Brighton station have tried to home in on Brighton's quirky nature by opening up a bar and restaurant called Oddsocks, where you can sip on a drink and be amazed by the crazy world that is a bar where the staff all wear odd socks. Far out, man!

A Miscellany of Munching –
Regional Fare and Local Dishes

Our county is known for its 'seven good things of Sussex', the first three of which, according to Revd Thomas Fuller in 1662, were Arundel grey mullet Pulborough eel, Chichester lobster and Selsey cockles. Rye herring, Amberley trout and 'Bourne (Eastbourne) wheatear (also known as the Orlatan) were added to the list by the author of *Spirit of the Downs*, Arthur Becket, nearly three centuries later (the name of this book is now shared with a Sussex vodka). Admiral Chambers, writing in 1936, added a Southdown saddle of mutton, a Patching truffle pie, a basket of Goring figs, a bunch of Worthing grapes and Worthing tomatoes and Downland mushrooms. If you've eaten all of those and are still hungry there are many more than fourteen good things, as Sussex is also known for Ashdown Partridge Pudding, Chiddingly Hot Pot, Sussex Bacon Pudding, Sussex Hogs' Pudding, Huffed Chicken, Sussex Churdles, Sussex Shepherds' Pie, Sussex Blanket Pudding, Sussex Smokies, Sussex Well Pudding, Sussex Drip Pudding and Chichester Pudding. The county record office in Chichester has copies of *Sussex County Magazine* dating from 1926 to 1956 that lists even more traditional Sussex recipes. You can find Eel Pudding, Plum Heavies, Sussex Beef Pudden, Potato and Cheese Cakes, Seed Cake, Lobster Pye and Fleed Cake, which can be washed down with Woodruff wine or the fruit-based Lamb's Wool. Finally, the Oakden website lists an old recipe for Sussex Hunter's Pudding; however, this seems similar to our other multitude of puddings.

There is no one dish that Sussex is known for in the same way as a Yorkshire pudding or Cornish pasty, but the nearest contender and the most delicious sweet dish here must be Sussex Pond Pudding. This is a mix of pastry, brown sugar, butter and lemon, which when steamed for several hours produces a 'pond' of buttery lemon juices on the surface and around the pudding as you demolish it. Sussex Pond Pudding is the 'best of all English boiled suet puddings' according to the late cookery writer Jane Grigson. It also very aptly appears in Florence White's 1932 compilation *Good Things in England*. It is have believed to have first appeared in Hannah Wolley's 1672 collection *The Queen-like Closet*, though early versions contain no lemon – Wolley suggested using apple or gooseberries. Not until Grigson's 1974 recipe does the desert include a whole lemon, which means that a sunny surprise awaits you as the beige-coloured suet pastry surrounding collapses. The dish has been through several redevelopments over the years, but still remains a great citrus-flavoured dish that warms and delights its eater, especially as the colder autumn nights draw in. Forty-odd years on and I can still clearly remember the taste of the lemon sponge pudding my primary school cook used to bake, and this dish is guaranteed to have an even longer-lasting effect. There is nothing finer than a soft, rich pastry case wrapped around and hiding a sweet, buttery fruit filling – no wonder Sussex puddings of this type have never gone out of fashion.

The roots of its name are mysterious. The Sussex Pond Pudding is sometimes claimed to be named after the dew ponds that decorate the top of the South Downs and provided hilltop-grazing cattle with much needed water from dew and rainfall. These ponds are believed by some to be how Jack and Jill in the nursery rhyme got their drink of water, rather than from a well. Dew ponds existed well before the first mention of them by name in 1865, and are likely to be from Saxon times in Wiltshire or even as ancient as Neolithic times if flint tools near them on the Downs are as of the same age. The eighteenth and nineteenth centuries saw a resurgence in their building as landlords continue to implement enclosure of their land, and it was around 1880 that H. J. Glover (who passed the recipe to Florence White) claimed he was given the recipe by Chailey, a nursemaid. Whatever their antiquity, it is possible this is what inspired the 'pond' part of the name, which grows as the suet exterior collapses. Should you not like lemon, then national treasure Mary Berry added apples to her recipe; some chefs add lime and *The Guardian*'s Felicity Cloake even added ginger. Adding raisins is how you get the 'Blackeyed Susan' we mentioned earlier.

Below is Florence White's recipe from 1932:

Make a good suet crust, put in some currants, and a little sugar.

Divide in two and roll each piece into a rather thick round.

Put into the middle of one round a ball of butter mixed with sugar, using the proportions of a 1/2 lb. butter to 1/4 lb. demerara sugar.

Gather up the edges of the crust, and enclose the butter ball securely by covering the join with the second round crust and pinching that up.

Put into a floured cloth, tie up rather tightly and boil 3 hours or more according to size.

Be careful, though, as Sussex puddings can kill you. But don't worry, it's only if you're a mythical Sussex creature called a Knucker Dragon. In ancient stories, these winged wonders lived in a number of deep holes filled with water, said by some to be bottomless. The Knucker Dragon of Lyminster was such a wrong'un that after a rampage of killing livestock and humans one story says that the monster aggravated the king of Sussex to such an extent that he offered his daughter's hand in marriage to any knight who could kill the beast. Consequently, a local character called Jim Pulk (or Puttock in some stories) fed the beast an indigestible Sussex pudding. While the dragon struggled with its stomach gripes Pulk put it to his sword, claiming a mayorship (usually said to be Arundel) as an additional prize.

Although sounding as indigestible as the pudding that killed the Knucker Dragon, Sussex Lardy Johns are one of the delicious cakes and biscuits Sussex is known for, along with Sussex Plum Heavies and, since 1972, banoffee pie. Creating a brand-new dessert must have been a challenge by the 1970s, but not as difficult it seems as finding a new fruit in Sussex. The Gage family of Firle Place were said to be the same Gages who introduced the greengage plum to our shores. Unfortunately, there seems to be no proof that this was the case, and it is now believed gages were not from brought into the country by the Gage family of Firle, despite the similar name. Talking of plums, it was also believed for many years that the first Victoria plum seedling was discovered in the village of Alderton in

Tremains Organic Cheddar. (Courtesy of High Weald Dairy)

Sussex. A spanner is thrown into the works of this story, unfortunately, when you realise we have no Alderton in Sussex. There is one, however, in Suffolk.

Moving on to the savoury dishes mentioned above, we start with the dish from this books's title: the Sussex Smokie. This is unusual for Sussex dishes (many of which are fairly unhealthy or use more frowned-upon ingredients) in that it is still regularly made by Sussex chefs. Our recipe here is kindly provided by Mark of High Weald Dairy of Horsted Keynes and their website for further fabulous recipes is at the end of the book.

Ingredients (serves 4 as a starter)
150 g Tremains organic cheddar
250 g smoked haddock
1 leek diced and sweated
2 tbsp chopped parsley and chives
150 ml double cream
150 ml whole milk
2 tsp butter and plain flour roux (half flour/half butter)
Handful of breadcrumbs

Method
Poach smoked haddock in milk and cream on gentle heat for 3–5 minutes. Sweat leeks until soft. Remove fish from milk and then add the roux to the liquid and reheat until thickened. Add 100g Tremains organic cheddar and mix well. Add herbs and leek and haddock. Mix 50g cheddar with breadcrumbs. Fill four ramekins with the haddock mixture and top with breadcrumbs and the cheddar. Bake for 10–15 minutes at 180°C. Serve with warm crusty bread or croutes. You could also place a poached quail's egg on top.

The only problem with the Smokie today is with the issue of reducing our 'food miles' and that of sustainability as the dish traditionally uses haddock, which is a deepwater fish, rarely found in these waters and so perhaps a twenty-first-century Smokie should use fish found off Sussex shores? The sea has different fish at different times of year, so we could even vary the Smokie throughout the year if we follow the advice of the Sporting Fish website. They explain that off Brighton's beaches in spring we see summer fish like mackerel and garfish making their way in. Common also at that time

Right: An anglers' festival on Brighton's Palace Pier in 1937. (Courtesy of RPAM BAH)

Below: Fishing market, Brighton seafront.

of year are plaice and flounders, which I personally think sounds like an estate agent when said in combination. In summer, Brighton beaches can provide bass, mackerel, thornback rays, sole, scad, garfish, smoothound, flounders, plaice, dogfish, mullet and, lastly, pout (yes, it's a fish). In the autumn fishermen tend to catch mackerel, bass and garfish in the day and then whiting, pout and sole in the evening. Finally, in the winter you may catch bass, pout, whiting, dabs and codling, which sound like the members of the Anthill Mob (for anyone of a certain age, that one).

Fish are obviously welcome to Sussex's coast at Brighton, but unbelievably there was another type of visitor that was welcomed as recently as 1985 to Brighton's dining rooms. Dogs were allowed to be in dining rooms until that year, until the Brighton and Hove Hotels, Guest Houses and Restaurants association banned them. Since then, of course, guide dogs have been the only exception. Doggie ice cream (ice cream for dogs, not made of them) has even been served at Highdown tea rooms, north-east of Worthing and the recently reopened café is still dog friendly.

Food lovers can try and eat their way around Sussex by visiting food-themed place names. Should you actually be able to eat the dish named in the place, then you deserve a well-earned pat on the back. Why not start with some ham and pea soup from Ham Lane, Lewes, and the more easterly Peasmarsh. The meat aspect of the dish may cause you to (go to) Burpham, however. Next, a main course of partridge from Partridge Green, baked in some apples from Appledram, all cooked in a Dripping Pan. A further main course could be some cod, cooked at Codmore Hill, near Pulborough, washed down with a nice glass of white wine from Wineham. For pudding, a choice of crumbles from Crumbles, near Langley Point, or Cake from Cakeham Manor. If it's Christmas then try Sproutes

Highdown House and gardens, a doggy destination for hungry hounds.

The Old Ship Hotel, home to medieval banquets.

Lane, near Coolham, which has its own Sage Cottage. Finally, don't forget to pay your bill at Billingshurst.

Before we finish, the ultimate historical food and drink crawl is nearby in our good county. You can drink across the dates and chomp your way through the centuries in Sussex if you know where to look. For medieval banquets you can try Herstmonceux Castle and then travel to Brighton for the cellars under the Old Ship for a private dining experience in the earliest days of Brighthelmstone (as Brighton was called until 1810). The cellars are built with stone from Normandy, suggesting they have been lined with stones from the walls of Brighton's monastery, which the French destroyed in 1514. The Old Ship also has a Tudor Room that was originally Brighton's post office until 1777. If you want a Tudor building for dining in West Sussex, then the Spread Eagle Hotel in Midhurst has rooms Queen Elizabeth allegedly visited. In the Stuart Age, Charles II was said to have dined at the George and Dragon in Houghton, and for a Victorian dining experience the Hilton Brighton Metropole's sumptuous high-ceilinged 1890 dining room is the only place to eat in surroundings designed by Alfred Waterhouse in the county. For Edwardian dining contact Preston Manor, and to experience the 1930s there is the Hummingbird Restaurant in the art deco

Preston Manor, location of Edwardian dining experiences.

Preston Manor drawing room.

Shoreham Airport, where the Hummingbird Restaurant lets you dine in 1930s surroundings.

Shoreham Airport building. For wartime dining, the Old Ship's cellars are also where Churchill was said to have held a wartime cabinet, so food would never have been far away where Churchill was concerned. Finally, for a Cold War-era setting that looked up to the stars just as the human race was, the Chartwell Suite at the Metropole was first built in the year of the Berlin Wall's construction as the Starlit Lounge. All this time-travelling tucker testing will leave you ready for a twenty-first-century sleep, but first we must return to the Middle Ages.

To finish our tour of Sussex food and drink past and present, I leave you with this taster of how the food and drink we still appreciate in Sussex today was once taken away from those who grew it as part of the feudal system. Today in Sussex food and drink is an industry thankfully produced by all classes and enjoyed by all of those in the county and our many visitors. With the focus increasing on healthy, nutritious, free-range, organic and locally produced food, a rural county like Sussex, which produces so much food for the nation, will continue to be a vital part of the nation's wellbeing.

Left: The Starlit Rooms, on top of the Metropole Hotel. Today the Chartwell Suite.

Below: The star designs in the bar area of the Starlit Rooms.

Starlit Rooms interior.

Sussex farming scene. (Courtesy
of RPAM BAH)

Bind Days in Bury
In the West Sussex village called Bury,
Long ago villagers were ordered to carry
'The Lorde's corne and cheese,
To Shoreham-By-Sea.
And when appointed to do so,
Any other place' they were bound to go.

And if this didn't make them broke;
'Of every house where issueth smoake,
The Lorde is to have one wood-henn,
At the Feast of Our Lord', and at Easter again.
Never one of said tenants, except 'Old Raulfe
May marry (his son, his daughter and himself)
Or sell horse and calf before showeth the Lorde,
Who may retain the same (at a price he can afford).'

'And the Lorde, so kindly (for his station)
Will let your hogs feed (for a consideration).'
Old England the days of ale and plenty?
Only if you were the landed gentry.

A final Sussex farming scene.
(Courtesy of RPAM BAH)

Acknowledgements

Thanks to Angeline and all at Amberley for commissioning me once more, putting up with my range of no doubt daft questions, and then editing and producing another smashing book. My thanks also to Mike Tristram at Sompting Estate for his pointing me to the Sussex Traditions website, and to the contributors there for letting me quote them. Thanks also to Paul at the Lewes Arms for his kind use of images and Miles Jenner of Harveys Brewery for his support and encouragement, as well as his kind offer of the launch for this book at the brewery. Mark at High Weald Dairy was especially generous with use of their images and recipe for a Sussex Smokie – you can work your way through their other irresistible recipes on the High Weald Dairy website overleaf. Rick and Kirsty Goring were also helpful with images and information about Wiston Estate, so thanks there too. Vanessa at Kent and Sussex Cottages kindly supplied images of the wonderful Piece of Cheese Cottage, and if you'd like to try a stay there the website is overleaf. Huge thanks to Martin Hayes of West Sussex Past for his permission to use images of Belloc and 'Bellocia Beacons' in this book. View around 18,000 photographs and pictures on free-to-use websites provided by West Sussex Record Office and the County Library Service. Just type 'West Sussex Past portal' in your search engine to find these databases and other local history websites. Kevin Bacon at the Royal Pavilion and Museums, Brighton and Hove Archive was his wonderful helpful self as always and I definitely owe you a pint, fellow 'Kev'. Alison Musk at the now sadly defunct *TASTE* magazine was her usual supportive self, but of course as always my biggest dollop of thanks and love go to my wife Laura and two boys Seth and Eddie for trying to ensure that despite writing about food and drink for a large part of this year I keep fit rather than fat.

Further Reading

For the Sussex Smokie recipe, and other charming cheesy dish recipes, visit High Weald's website: www.highwealddairy.co.uk/recipes
To stay in the Piece of Cheese: www.kentandsussexcottages.co.uk/coastal-sussex/hastings-and-st-leonards-cottages/rh1088-the-piece-of-cheese

For another past Pond Pudding recipe and for others such as Sussex Heavies (which are actually quite light): https://oakden.co.uk/?s=sussex

For a treasure trove of old recipes and food being mentioned: www.foodsofengland.co.uk; sussextraditions.org; www.facebook.com/sussextraditions; www.cookipedia.co.uk/recipes_wiki/Category:Sussex_cheeses; www.sportingfish.co.uk/venues/east-sussex/brighton-and-hove-beaches.html

Two archives I thoroughly recommend are Royal Pavilion and Museums, Brighton and Hove and West Sussex Past: http://185.121.204.173/PastPictures/Default.aspx?

Belloc, Hilaire, *The Four Men: A Farrago* (1911)
Candlin, Lilian, *Tales of Old Sussex* (Countryside Books, 1992)
Cooke, Arthur Stanley, *Off the Beaten Track In Sussex* (Herbert Jenkins, 1911)
Milligan, Spike, *Adolf Hitler: My Part In His Downfall* (Michael Joseph Ltd, 1971)
Moore, J., *Sussex Recipes* (James Pike Ltd, 1976)
Muggleton, David, *Brewing in West Sussex* (Amberley Publishing, 2017)
Wilson, A. N., *Hilaire Belloc: A Biography* (Mandarin, 1997)

ALSO BY THE AUTHOR

A–Z of Brighton and Hove
Brighton and Hove In 50 Buildings
Celebrating Brighton and Hove
Lewes Pubs
Secret Brighton
50 Gems of Sussex
Historic England: Sussex
Historic England: Brighton and Hove

UPCOMING

A–Z of Worthing
Clock Towers of England